HOW TO GET THE KICK-ASS CAREER YOU DESERVE

GET THE RIGHT CV, MINDSET AND LINKEDIN APPROACH TO GIVE YOU THE EDGE!

Rebecca Pay

Publisher: Pay for Precision Publishing
ISBN: 978-1-7399932-0-7
Cover Design: Rebecca Pay
Illustrator: Rebecca Pay
Formatter: Claire Jennison
Editor: Kirsten Rees

Connect with the author:
www.payforprecision.com
LinkedIn: https://www.linkedin.com/in/payforprecision/
Facebook: https://www.facebook.com/PayforPrecision
Twitter: https://twitter.com/PayforPrecision

CONTENTS

I would like to dedicate this book to my late grandparents, without your genes I could not have written it.
I hope this book would have made you all proud.

FOREWORD

By Dan Meredith, author of *How To Be F*cking Awesome*

Finding a job in a post pandemic world has become a truly challenging problem (especially if you are now totally unemployable like myself). Finding a way to not only stand out amongst the vast sea of candidates is one thing, but what if you feel trapped? What if you think the path you're on is the only path available to you? What if you lie in bed at night thinking 'is this it?'

That's why I am so proud of what Rebecca has created. Should I ever be in a position where I need to write a CV, polish up LinkedIn and completely change the direction of my life, she is one of a handful of people in the last ten years of business I would recommend. Because not only can you (if you follow her advice) get the next job, but you can position yourself in a way to GET THE JOB YOU NEVER THOUGHT YOU COULD.

Back when I was employed, this is something I NEVER thought was possible - I thought that once you have set out on your career path, that's your lot.

Rebecca and her system have shown me - and will show you too - that is not the case.

So take your time to read this book, apply the lessons and - in time - marvel at how your life can change with her advice.

Good luck!

INTRODUCTION

What will this book give you?

This book is a guide on how to change your life. That's a pretty big statement, isn't it?

Work is such a big part of our lives. If you are able to pivot your career or take a step up, this will have a significant impact on your whole life. Maybe you have felt stuck in a crappy, humdrum role for too long or just maybe the big corporate job isn't lighting your fire anymore and you want to do something that really makes a difference.

I'm here to tell you, you CAN do it and not only that, but I'll show you how. This book is a mixture of a practical guide on how to create a CV and use LinkedIn to find work as well as getting your mindset aligned with your goal.

I will also help you work out what this goal actually is in the first place as maybe you know you want to change, but you're not really sure what you want to do.

How to use this book:

Each chapter states what it is about at the start, and you may not need to read every chapter as some will relate more closely to your situation than others. So, feel free to pick and choose chapters, they pretty much all work as standalone entities. You may also wish to re-read some chapters as you start on your journey and get stuck at certain points.

To view full size pdfs of the images from chapter 2 please go to https://payforprecision.com/cv-examples/ to download your free copies.

My Kick-ass CV template is also available for free at www.payforprecision.com

Please note, all the advice for CVs or resumes in this book is primarily aimed at UK-based people but it will also apply to the US for the most part, as they have remarkably similar expectations for resumes or CVs.

If you're from another country or applying for roles outside the UK, please check the local guidance for writing CVs as there will be different expectations such as a need for a photo or personal information. Do your research because although most of the information in this book will still apply, just beware of the technical CV advice if you are not applying for a role in the UK.

It should also be noted, I am a *little bit sweary* at times and if you're easily offended this book might not be for you.

CHAPTER 1
WHAT JOB DO YOU REALLY WANT – PIVOT INTO PERFECTION

Why no one is trapped

Let's get stuck straight in, maybe you feel suffocated in your current situation and don't know what you want to do. Read on.

You may have always planned to be in the career you're in now. Perhaps you studied for it at school, started an apprenticeship or just got in there early. Perhaps you just fell into a job or followed its natural progression, and you are where you are now, without any planning. Either way, once you've been in an industry or a sector, or a particular job for some time, it can feel quite claustrophobic and as if you're trapped.

Now if it was always part of your big plan to be in this role, and things are going according to plan, then bravo. This chapter isn't for you. This one is for people who are worried they are trapped in their current career and scared they can't get out, or it is too late to change. As young as thirteen at school, we have to make choices about subjects which could potentially have a long-term impact on our careers.

It's drummed into us that the decisions we make then will impact the rest of our lives. Yes, they do for a while but frankly, you can do GCSEs at any age. And after a certain point, they're not that relevant anyway. So, you can pick up a new career at nearly any age.

I've recently heard of someone who was aged eighty-four graduating. This is epic. You maybe don't want to wait until your eighties to get a degree if that's something on your bucket list, or a need for your next career move. But it is never too late.

No one is trapped because there are always choices to make. You can retrain from scratch, if you have to. There are ways and means of gathering transferable skills, perhaps studying alongside your current job which may mean a couple of years of really hard work, but don't ever call yourself totally trapped, even if you've done the same career for thirty years because it just isn't true.

If there's a dream job for you – perhaps you want to learn how to dive and set up a diving school on an island - then go and do it!

There may be reasons in your life meaning you CHOOSE not to do this because you have family or other responsibilities. But at the end of the day it doesn't make you trapped, it's you making choices. Always remember, everything is a choice.

For example, it may seem as if there is no choice because you feel obliged to care for a loved one, but when you think about it, you're not, because you love that person and that's why you want to care for them. In fact, it may be that earning more money would enable the level of care to be far better. Worth remembering.

I work to make my business a great success as I know my daughter, who is autistic, will need some private support as she grows up, and I want to be able to provide this. I never thought it would be possible until I started to believe in myself and realised I could choose to take that path.

I realise every situation and financial setup is complicated, so it can be easy for me to say you're not trapped in a situation when you might feel it. But usually, there is a way out and believing you CAN get out is often half the battle.

The point is to remember everything you do is a choice. And just because you chose to follow a certain career path, doesn't mean you have to stay on it. Once you truly know what you want to do, you can focus on finding out how to get there. But where do you start?

What DON'T you want to do?

Sometimes, the easiest way to work out what we do want to do is by working out what we don't. It's something I often ask clients, why do you want to leave this job, what do you really dislike about it? Think about the things in your current role that don't sit right with you, or that you don't enjoy. Think about those tasks, those styles of work, the cultures you've disliked working in.

Culture is so important, it has such a big impact on our daily working lives. I work for myself, so I create the culture I'm in, it is down to me. If it's not a nice working atmosphere, it's because I've created that for myself. I currently only work with remote people anyway, so I don't have a day-to-day situation, although I do share an office with a friend.

But what don't I want to do? I don't ever want to be in a big busy office full of other people, even if I grew my business where I had other employees, I definitely don't want to be sat in an office with them all day, it would do my head in. It's just not me, I feel more relaxed by myself some of the time.

So, think about this for yourself, for example, if you hate shift work, retraining as a nurse is probably not going to be a good plan for you. Although having said that, perhaps you can work as a nurse in a GP's practice because their shifts are always going to be daytime and rarely weekends. So, decide what you definitely don't want, and this will help bring you closer to what you do want.

Which roles match your ethos? Open your mind

Many companies have a strong ethos or ethics. But first, you need to think about what yours are. You're allowed to change your mind as well. The ethics, and the moral standards you had when you were twenty-one, may be very different to where you are now. Or maybe you're twenty-one now, and you have really strong views on things, expect them to change. An open and flexible mind is far more useful in life than a very rigid one. If you have a very fixed view of something this may cause you problems. It's useful to be able to be open to new ideas and to listen to other viewpoints.

Over time, we often change our minds about things. As you grow older, and perhaps have children, this can really change your view of the world in which you live. It certainly changes your mind about priorities in your life. Things like working all the hours, commuting and earning big money may become less important if you have a young family to look after and care for, because you want to spend time with your children and watch them growing up, or perhaps you want to work harder to provide them with the best. Either way, it is not just about you anymore.

So, what do I mean by your ethics or your ethos? Think about what your view of the world is, do you think we should all be kind, do you think we should look after people or do you think you should be looking after yourself? Do you just work very hard to care for your family or do you want to work hard so that it helps other people as well? There is no right or wrong answer here by the way. There may be a trendy answer, but I'm not here to judge you, whatever your true morals are, that's what you need to be working towards. Then you'll find in general you'll feel much happier and less anxious as a person.

There's peace to be found if your actions in your everyday life match what you feel and believe deep inside. Anxiety and unhappiness often stem from a disparity between the two. This can sometimes happen with roles, because you end up in a job role where you're doing something you don't really believe in.

I'll give you an example here. I worked in advertising years ago for quite some time. It was great fun. We used to get loads of money to go out with clients, free lunches, free drinks, great bonuses. We worked really hard, but we also played hard. I had clients who were in the public sector and third sector, so this was great because I felt like I really wanted to work with charities and councils. I'd come from a newspaper background in a sales role, but the new role was more about building client relationships, it felt like a great role for me and a great fit. But I left!

When it came down to it, the ethos of the company didn't sit well with me. It turned out what we were trying to do a lot of the time, was rip these people off.

We had to upsell them to things like using full colour in the Guardian. I would then negotiate with my friend Dan at the Guardian who I built a relationship with, to give me free colour on that page. So, I would charge the client the £400 for the colour on their advert and the company pocketed the difference. We all got a percentage of it as part of our bonus. So, there was quite an incentive there.

The job seemed great as I was working with the clients I wanted but the underhandedness started to make me feel uncomfortable and I began to find myself quite miserable at work. So, if you start to get like that, work out why, and then make the move.

Don't be scared to get away from a job that's making you feel uncomfortable or sad on some level. The time to move is now.

Don't wait for another ten years.

What will your legacy be?

When you look back, what do you want to remember about your time on earth? What do you want to remember about your working life? Do you want it to have been a corporate slog smashing your way to the top and crushing people on the way, or do you want to feel you made a real difference, even if that's developing others underneath you and giving people a chance to fulfil their potential?

Whatever it is, if your current job isn't fulfilling that need, then go about finding it. This book will help you discover not only what you want to do, but how you can achieve it. Using your CV, as well as some other tools.

There are certain jobs that we fall into. They are good for a while in your twenties. Even in your thirties you can feel like you're doing well, and it's working for you, you're getting paid plenty and life is good. As you get older, that might not feel the same, you want to actually make a difference with what you're doing and make an impact on the world.

Now this doesn't have to be a Mother Teresa type moment where you're working for nothing, or for a company that only works with homeless people, (it might be one of those things), but let's not confuse ourselves here. Legacy can be many things, making a difference, and finding a company that makes a difference, doesn't mean it's a company that isn't making money or isn't corporate.

There are many corporate brands now using much better ethics and who have a really strong work culture and a focused approach on making a difference in the world.

Pixar are well known for their ethical approach and attitude towards social responsibility.

"On one side is making art for art's sake. On the other, is the pure commercial side - films made to follow a trend. If you go entirely for the art side, at some point you fail economically. If you go to the commercial side, you fail from a soul point of view. There is somewhere in the middle."

- Ed Catmull, Co-founder and former President of Pixar.

This shows that companies can still be successful, AND ethical. It doesn't mean you've got to take a massive drop in salary just to find a job that makes a difference. You may wish to take a drop in salary if you've already earned enough, which is fine. But don't confuse the two. They don't necessarily come hand in hand.

So, what do you think your legacy is going to be? Have a look around and think about the kind of difference you could make with the skills you've got. There are all sorts of things - you may want to lobby the government or make amendments at a national level to change things for people in your industry. Your dream employer may give opportunities in a more diverse way or employ homeless people, or ex-convicts? It might be important to know your company gives a percentage back or supports the local community. Would you push the customer-led approach? As a client of mine does by working very high up in an international telecoms company (he on-shored all the call centres back to the UK and decreased complaints tenfold!).

The options are virtually endless really, but think about what is important to YOU.

What does the future look like?

Can you picture yourself in a new role somewhere doing something you really enjoy? What are you doing, where do you work? Who do you work with? What do you come home to? What's your family setup, where are you living, how much money do you earn? What do you do at weekends, where do you go on holiday?

Planning what your future may look like is not only fun, it's the best way of setting really achievable goals. It sometimes feels difficult to picture an exact future. And obviously, there are no guarantees, we never know what life might throw at us and we have to roll with the punches. But having a clear plan of what you want your future to look like will help you work out how the hell to get there. If you've really got absolutely no idea, it's going to be a lot harder to make a plan to get there, isn't it?

Now thinking about how you FEEL when you're in that future will also really help you think about how happy you might be in that new role. Perhaps you're hoping to find a new relationship as well. If you're in a happier place, you might be more open to finding a relationship.

Your daily work life has a big impact on the rest of your life. I'm not saying if you get a dream job then you will find your dream partner, of course not. However, it's more likely that if you're doing something you are really aligned with then you'll be relaxed and happy, and someone good will come into your life. Because the more you, you can be, the more you attract the right sort of people into your life as friends, or partners, or colleagues.

Do things now that your future self will thank you for, of course give yourself time to rest, but if now's the time to knuckle down and work hard for this new career, then do it, you will thank yourself later.

Research and plan

Once you decide on what career move you're making and what the ideal job is, (maybe it's just a step up from the job you're already doing), researching and planning is the next step.

Now, I'm no expert on every career, clearly, and there is specific career help out there. But once you've got an ideal job role in mind, you can investigate what qualifications and skills you need to get them.

Now, the first thing to do usually is to Google the job, look for job descriptions, and job adverts for that role and that will tell you what they're looking for. So, do you need a degree? Do you need certain qualifications? What skills are they looking for? What experience do you need? Look at a few because some will have different expectations. Combine that information together. And look at which of those things you need to get. One would hope you have some of the skills, that's why you want to do that role in the first place. But whatever they are, build on those skills.

Perhaps you need to be able to coach or manage people better - work on doing that in your current role. Perhaps you need to take a qualification. If you need your PRINCE2 or whatever it is, then go ahead and get it. It might be something where you need a Maths GCSE or an English GCSE. Whatever it is, work out how you can achieve it.

Once you've got the list of things that you need, then you can look at how to get them. Local councils offer adult education. These can be ways to top up skills or you can do things like bookkeeping qualifications, I previously did that myself as an adult education course of an evening.

The sooner you can research all of this and start planning how you're going to get there, the better. Obviously, it's hard for me to give really specific examples here because you could be reading this and be jumping from one career to another and there is a myriad of possibilities.

However, there are some general tips to help you plan it out.

Getting that clear plan and not panicking is really important. It might feel overwhelming if you look at it all and realise they all require a degree. Firstly, if that's the case, do more research, check more job titles and check that is always true. Then talk to someone. Find someone who does that job already if you can.

Places like LinkedIn are great for this, build up a relationship with someone or just ask for some help in a post. Speak to people in those roles. Check. If they 100% always need that degree then you need to look into where you can get into a degree course for it.

This can become a little overwhelming, but doesn't make it impossible. It's still doable. Study can be done part-time alongside a current job, or you could go all in and do it in a couple of years. Big ask? Hell yes, but if that's what you really want to do and focus on, it's still possible.

It may be something far simpler and a case of assessing your current skills. But whichever it is, get that plan in place so you can break it down into actionable steps, then start!

Have you got transferable skills?

You may be making a big career move that involves retraining or study, but obviously for smaller changes that don't involve huge qualifications, there are ways to gain the skills you need. Voluntary work is a great way to gather skills and experience of things you haven't quite got.

You can also think about your current role. Is there any way of expanding it or doing extra work in other departments to build up that repertoire you need? If you're offering to do stuff without asking for a pay rise, in order to further yourself, there's no reason they'll say no. Most places will be interested in developing you professionally and personally. Some places offer a mentoring scheme. And any good place of work will support you in retraining or help you develop yourself.

Don't rule this out, speak to someone at work that you trust.

You also need to look at your current skills and look at how transferable a lot of them are. There might be some roles you've done already where you have built up things like customer service experience, project managed something for the local school, kept records or even created designs as a hobby or as a volunteer.

Don't be afraid to describe a previous role on your CV by focusing on the skills you are looking to highlight. For example, you may have done a role that involved administration, but you want to showcase project management on your CV. Elements of the administration role will still be applicable like organisation, planning or meeting deadlines. This is just an example, but I'm sure you understand what I am saying here, think about all the different areas of the role and the skills that you might have developed.

In any role that involved dealing with clients or customers you will have built skills in customer service and communication, and these are highly transferable to lots of other roles even if the client is completely different or if you are changing industry. Communication is pretty much key in everything, so highlighting this as a skill is nearly always important. Sometimes people don't realise how transferable their skills are until they write it all down. So do just that and think about your skills as objectively as possible, ask for help from someone who knows you or works with you if necessary.

It's not selfish to choose the hard route

When you've worked out exactly what you want to do and found the route to get there, it might feel selfish. Perhaps the route is not going to be easy, you may have to go back to uni, retrain in some way, maybe have to start at the bottom and take a massive salary cut. This may impact family or a partner, if you've got one. It might mean having to downscale where you live or put on hold plans to move to a bigger place, maybe even cut out holidays for a while, whatever it is you might be making sacrifices, and you will be expecting someone else in your life to make some sacrifices too.

If you choose this hard route remember it's okay to be selfish sometimes, because at the end of the day it is your life. Now I'm not saying that means we don't consider what the people around us want or need. Of course, we do. But ultimately, long term it will be better for them too.

Obviously, plan it carefully and discuss it with a partner. Putting yourself first, in this situation is important as well, because finding a job true to you and what you believe in is going to be brilliant for them in the long run.

You will be a happier, better person to be around.

Perhaps you've been miserable in a corporate job, commuting, doing long hours. I have spoken to plenty of clients who were earning shed loads but deep down they were miserable, and that always comes out somewhere. Unhappiness shows even if we put on a positive front to the world. Arguing with a partner, snapping at the kids, not being much fun at weekends, or perhaps even working through them. I have been there!

Now, you might end up putting in extra work in order to change a career, I realise that, but putting in that hard work for a couple of years to have the long term gain of being in a job you really love will be worth it. And even if it doesn't work out, let's not kid ourselves. Sometimes things don't work out or you might change your mind. You will know you gave it your best shot and that is so important.

The last thing you want to do is be old and grey, ninety years old, sat in your armchair, looking back, wishing you had given something a go or retrained to be something that you really wanted to be. Have a long hard look at what you want, have a plan, and of course, discuss it with your family if you have one, but don't be scared to go for the hard route.

It will pay off.

Cut out the noise

This relates to the last section and it's about cutting out what everyone else wants. Now, I don't mean this in a negative way, and that you should completely ignore what your partner or family really need or want. Obviously, big decisions about income, or maybe even relocating etc. do need to be made as a family, to an extent. What I mean is, make sure you get time alone to think about what YOU really want to do.

Make that time for yourself, go for long walks, maybe even take some time off, go away for a day or two or a weekend, you might be in a position where you can take a week off, get away from everyone and everything. Make sure you're making the decision based on what YOU really want, not what everyone else wants.

It's great to take advice from others, but sometimes this can really cloud our own judgement. Sometimes people are too quick to ask other people what they think. Personally, I'm not, I very rarely ask anyone for advice, as anyone who knows me will know. This can sometimes be a bad thing because I can bumble along, and actually I could have got a really good idea from someone, but often it's because I'm quite self-sufficient and I know I can find the answers myself.

Believe in yourself, you know, deep down what you really want to do. Now, if you need some help to achieve your goals by all means, ask for some help, but asking for help to make the decision, I advise against it! My real advice here is to dig deep, have those long walks and have those hard conversations with yourself. Get to the point where you definitely know what you want to do, then you can work out how to get there. Don't worry about the details until you decide what you really want first, then find a sensible way to get there, that works for you.

Maybe try journalling, hand-writing your thoughts on paper can be really useful. Maybe voice note it or just get it out of your brain onto some paper and see how you feel about it. Going for walks while listening to music and getting time out in nature, is one of the things that really helps me with this sort of stuff. I actually wrote a pros and cons list when I was deciding whether or not to leave my ex-husband. Just me, alone in the pub, with some music in my ears.

I wrote a list of pros and cons down on a pad of paper. I only had one pint first as I don't think making decisions drunk is something I would advocate! It was personal and just for me.

Ultimately, the deciding factor was I couldn't risk losing the chance to be with someone I had fallen in love with. We had met on Twitter and once in real life (the day before I did the list), so I had to decide what to do. We have now been married for ten years and have two children, so I guess you could say it was the right decision!

I find driving also helps me think sometimes, often just sitting at home doesn't work so well, but obviously you do what works for you. Generally taking time out in a space away from where you live your everyday life, is the best way to do some proper thinking. However you do it, cut out all that noise around you and find some space to listen to yourself and what you really want.

CHAPTER 2
STRUCTURE – 'THE PERFECT CV'

Where do I start?

Once you have a job aim, you can think about your CV. If you picked up this book for the CV help, bingo, the next two chapters coming up are for you!

Firstly there is NO perfect CV (sorry, bubble burst!), it will depend on you and what the AIM of that CV is. Working through other chapters will help you decide what role you are going for, but this chapter is the technical advice on how to structure a CV.

Most people start with their old CV, probably one you did at school or just after uni and you have perhaps added to it over the years.

Firstly, don't ever just update an old CV. Try and look at it with fresh eyes and see it as a brand-new entity. Use the info you have gathered over the years on the old CV, but don't just throw on another page and add more and more.

In this chapter, I work through the structure I use when I create a CV. It is tried and tested and more importantly, it is easy to read and logical in its approach. If you follow this structure, you will be off to a great start! Adapt it as you see fit according to your skills and experience.

Think about how you view a CV, is it legible, are the fonts common and readable, are there big chunks of unappealing text? Please, also try and keep it brief. Two pages is more than enough for the average person. Maybe three if you have a lot of training or courses that are relevant or if two is just too big a squash ... but be brutal as less is more.

Remember your CV is a highlights reel of your career, just enough to get them interested and wanting to interview you! Showing your journey but it is not a life story.

Please note that this advice is based on my professional experience and also not aimed at the creative industry. If you are a creative then you will probably want to highlight your skills and make yourself a more impressive CV and work on a portfolio as well. But if you are applying online then do be aware that large companies and recruiters do often use ATS for any type of role so having a simple version is often useful. When applying direct, or to smaller firms it won't be an issue.

Contact details and links

This seems so obvious, contact details are simple right? Well, they are but people still get them wrong, so it doesn't hurt to remind you of the basics.

Use an email address that doesn't make you look like a muppet. Whilst a hilarious Hotmail name might have been great when you first set it up, ensure you have a more sensible one, preferably with your name, for your CV.

And it goes without saying, but do make sure you check it regularly or have it forwarded to your main email. You can also have it set as a hyperlink, (right-click with the mouse whilst highlighting the text and click add link).

Put your mobile number on. Yes, you may get a few touting calls from recruiters plying their services, but it is a necessary form of contact in this day and age. Landlines are not usually necessary or expected.

Add your location, not your full address. Think about it, you are not going to sit waiting for the postman to deliver a job reply by snail mail, it just doesn't happen anymore. When you get a job offer and they need your full address, provide it then. Your CV may be posted on job boards and spreading your address around just isn't necessary.

Make sure you have a link to your LinkedIn profile (unless you really don't want to use LinkedIn). Love it or loathe it, LinkedIn is growing hugely and now has over 756 million users. This is the place to be for job opportunities and networking (see chapter 5) so make sure you have a LinkedIn account. More on how to set up your profile in a later chapter, but providing a link (again use a hyperlink and have the visible text just as LinkedIn) to your profile will help recruiters or employers find you on there. As they will go looking either way.

Profile summary

This section, which is sometimes titled profile and sometimes summary, is basically your elevator pitch. It needs to encapsulate who you are, why you are doing what you do and what impact you can and have had on a business.

Now, this all varies massively depending on your sector or industry and your personality. But as it is likely to be the first and possibly only part of your CV read in full (skim reading is a major skill requirement for recruiters) then you want to get it right.

I usually write this part last when doing a CV for a client and I would advise you to do the same. Try to avoid too many clichéd phrases and think about words that sound like you. **It is perfectly possible to have a professional CV that still contains some personality** and using interesting adjectives can help with this.

The best way to start though, is to brainstorm some ideas. Speak to colleagues, friends, a partner, and get them to describe you. Read old appraisals or reviews from clients and managers. Remind yourself on how you lead, what your approach is, how you are perceived by others and what you have achieved. What do you bring to a team or workplace and why is what you do better or different to anyone else?

Coming up with a USP (unique selling point) is really useful here. And it is why I suggest writing the profile last, as by then you will have reminded yourself of all the great things you have done and had time to think about the great things you want to do next. Having a why is powerful, so if you want to work somewhere to make a difference or you pursued your career as it was a childhood dream, don't be afraid to say so.

A great CV stands out because it is about the individual and is unique, not because it is fluorescent orange and has a photo of you doing the splits!

What is your USP and how to inject personality

As mentioned above, finding your USP for your CV profile is really important as this is something that will help you stand out against other candidates. Think about what you do differently from anyone else. Your USP is that thing that makes you unique, something that you do that no one else can. It can be hard to think of sometimes, so talking to people you have worked with or who know you well in the workplace can really shed some light on this.

You want your CV to sound like you, not just a generic CV for anyone who does your role. Don't be afraid to inject some personality into your CV, you can still keep things professional, but if you are very outgoing, friendly or energetic this should be coming across on your CV. If the CV reads in a boring way, then people will assume you are boring.

It is essential to be true to yourself here. If you are a fairly straight-forward character who just gets on with things that's totally cool, write it like it is you, don't be something you're not. But if you are a larger-than-life character please make sure your CV sounds like you. This really helps you find the right culture fit for you, so think about the type of business you want to work for and the kind of energy you want around you.

How to get this across on a CV is another matter as people do struggle with it. It is essentially why I have a business as I am really good at it! But I would advise using the profile to get some personality across and think about using different adjectives to the norm. Think of words that describe you and think of different ways to explain your style or approach.

If you are an extrovert don't be afraid to say it using words like dynamic, energetic, forward-thinking, infectious personality - all of these are perfectly acceptable, but obviously you need to find the words that work for you.

The aim is that when someone reads the CV, they get to know you a bit. So, give it to a friend to read and see if they think it sounds like you, this will give you a good idea of how well you have done it.

Key skills/competencies

Whether you call them skills or competencies they are a great section to have on the CV just under your profile. The first page needs to capture someone's attention and if they have to go hunting for your skills amongst your career experience it can be hard work. As people are often looking through dozens if not hundreds of CVs, let's make it easy for them to pick you. Super easy, barely an inconvenience (shout out to Ryan George fans, check out his screen pitches on YouTube, hilarious).

By having those key skills on that first page they are obvious and easy to read. There are a few ways to display them, but I tend to either list many in 2 or 3 columns (using tabs to create the columns) or choose 5 or 6 key areas and write them in bold – then write a little about each one next to each heading.

This gives you a chance to give examples of how you display those skills as well as space to expand and include more keywords. I talk about keywords in chapter 4, in essence, these are the words associated with the job you are going for. So in a job description or person spec. they are the skills and experience required to be chosen for interview. Adjust the skills section in line with each application.

Make sure your skills are at the expected level for the job you are applying for, for example having experience of Microsoft Office is not really a skill you need to mention when going for a finance director role.

The whole CV needs to be written in line with your target role, so if you are aiming at senior leadership roles then talk about strategic decisions making and leadership skills and show your understanding of not just your industry but of people and how to manage them.

Two layout examples for skills

KEY SKILLS

Relationship Building	Communication	Strategy
Technical and Commercial	Process Gap Analysis & Improvement	Problem Solving and Resolution
Analytical	Solution Design and Deployment	ERP, CRM, SFA, HRIS Applications
Onboarding & Enablement	Project & Programme Management	Change Management
Full Cycle Training Consultancy	Virtual & Classroom Delivery Trainer	Tenacity and Resilience
Implementation and Adoption	Integrity and Judgement	

KEY SKILLS

- **Leadership** – Collaborative, honest leadership with tailored performance management and coaching skills.
- **Team Development** – Devising training plans, supporting through coaching and succession planning.
- **Business Strategy** – Strategic planning and approach to delivering improved business performance.
- **Communication** – Excellent communication, networking, presentation, and customer service skills.
- **Commercial Awareness** – Astute business and commercial awareness with a vast breadth of experience.
- **Financial Control** – Highly experienced in the financial management control of multi-million-pound budgets.
- **Human Resources** – A broad understanding of a wide range of HR policies and procedures.
- **Organisation & Productivity** – Highly organised, skilled in developing a high productivity work environment.

Career highlights

This section is optional, as it does depend on your length of career and your target role, but it is ideal for showing off 2-4 of your best achievements ahead of your career history.

Creating a section for them means they will not get lost in your CV or forgotten about, and it also gives you a chance to shout about achievements that are most relevant to the job you are applying for. It is an ideal area to tweak and amend when you apply for jobs. Because of course, you will be amending your CV for every application, won't you? (see chapter 4 Tailor and Tweak).

Don't waffle on though, remember people do not need every detail of a project to understand if it was a success and the impact you had on it. The highlighted version is good enough and any details can be discussed at interview. It just needs to be enough to make them interested and to show the level of influence you have had in previous roles.

You do have the option to add in something non-work related, perhaps based on a voluntary role or an award you won, as long as it is relevant to your ideal role and the skills required for it.

If you have had a short career or don't feel you have enough to put in this section, then just leave it out.

Career history

The most common question I get asked is how far back do I go with my work history? Ten to fifteen years is sufficient. Summarise old roles in one sentence, things older than this old may not even need to be on there. Use some judgement here, showing you started as an apprentice twenty-five years ago can add to your journey and makes sense on the CV as a whole, just don't add any details about it (employer and dates are enough).

But if you did a paper round in 1995, it can be left off.

Have your employer, job title and the dates all in bold, ideally in a line, as you don't want to take up too much space, and try to line up all the headings down the page. Tabs are your friend here. There is no real necessity to include any information about the company. Your CV should be talking about you, not the places you worked for.

However, adding information that gives an idea of scale is really useful. Things such as the number of staff you managed, the size of budgets, projects, P&L, turnover etc. if relevant to your role.

As for what to put in the information, firstly, use bullet points. Large chunks of text are really hard to consume and off-putting to the reader. Secondly, ensure it is achievement based and not just a list of responsibilities. Try not to repeat words like responsible for, delivered, etc. Use plenty of action words but mix them up and focus on areas you made an impact on.

Whatever you do for a job, try and find some facts and figures to back up your achievements. Perhaps you made 15% of savings or increased sales by 40%, even better use the actual monetary amounts if you can. **Just remember that the highlights of your achievements are what you want to include, you don't need every detail of how you go there, that is for the interview**.

What you want is more information in the most relevant roles to the type of jobs you are going for. This will usually be the most recent roles. You shouldn't have huge amounts of information under older roles, unless you are going back to something you used to do. And even then, it is prudent to try and show how you have gained experience in those areas more recently if you can.

If you wish to keep in older roles, just keep the dates, employer and job title and have them listed, but don't feel you have to do this further back than fifteen or even ten years unless it is required (public sector roles will usually want all the roles listed, but usually have application forms anyway).

Education and training

This will be very individual and will rely entirely on what your actual education and training is of course! Any qualifications and education that is relevant should be here. Degree and above usually, when it comes to standard education, unless you are very young, a school leaver or graduate it is unlikely you need your GCSEs and A Levels.

However, if they are asking for GCSE Maths and English for example, of course include them. I have seen CEOs with GCSEs on their CVs and that is clearly unnecessary. Once you have a degree, anything before it isn't very relevant and if you have plenty of work experience the same applies.

Training wise, use some common sense, if the courses are related to what you do then include them, don't waste space listing every internal course ever completed. Some things will be great to include, for example, mental health first aid.

If your education history is sparse or non-existent, don't panic. Certainly don't lie. Most people have completed some form of training and including it shows a commitment to continuous professional development. There is no need to include information about what units were studied during a degree etc. (unless you are a graduate/student), just course names, provider if known and dates if you want to.

There is no real obligation to include dates as it will, of course, give an indication of your age. Age discrimination is against the law but that is for a reason and potentially it could be a factor in selection even subconsciously, so bear it in mind if it is something that concerns you.

Voluntary work

This is a great section if you have done any form of voluntary work in your life. It shows you care and have more interests outside of work. You may consider a temporary or contract role to gain experience or get your foot in the door, like the client below.

Case Study
Evolving an Opportunity

Shane came to me just before Christmas with an essay long CV of 5 pages and needed something that would get him some interviews. He knew what he had wasn't good enough. We got to work and spoke on the phone, and after some work on my part we got it down to 2 pages which summarised him and his skillset perfectly with no waffle. Plus a new LinkedIn profile.

He got a new position within a couple of months and recently let me know it has now become permanent. Getting that opportunity was the first step to a great new role!

In his own words:
"Rebecca was referred to me for CV writing and to put it simply, just "Wow!". I couldn't be more pleased with the end result. She produced a slick and punchy 2 page script from the information I provided and an hour on the phone in a matter of days. Pay for Precision is a very apt business name, you get exactly that, and I now have a Kick-Ass CV!"

It can also be a powerful area for gaining experience and transferable skills if you want to change career. Taking on voluntary work for a charity or school etc. can be a great way to grow in a field you want experience in. Or it can be a great way to give back, sharing your skills with places that cannot afford to pay for them.

Lots of charities have opportunities to work for them in voluntary roles. I have worked at the local hospital, a nature reserve and for the Citizens Advice Bureau over the years. The options are endless.

This website has a list of websites you can use to search for UK-based volunteer roles:

https://www.ncvo.org.uk/ncvo-volunteering/i-want-to-volunteer

Remember that coaching a local team, being on the PTA or a governor for a school, or doing anything community based without pay, all count as voluntary work. If you are lacking in career experience, voluntary work can be extended to show your skills and responsibilities accordingly, don't be afraid to adapt your CV into a format that suits you!

Interesting interests

Interests are sometimes a contentious issue. And my rule of thumb is add them if they are interesting. Now this isn't complicated, think about your interests objectively. Going for walks, reading and cooking may be things you love, but they aren't very interesting.

Harsh but fair!

If you have run marathons, been a pro skier, or have a really unusual or brilliant skill or hobby then by all means talk about it. But don't list a lot of dull past times as CV space is precious. Think about your CV as real estate and every square inch is valuable. Don't waste any space on anything unless it is selling you as the brilliant person you are.

Interesting interests can be a great talking point at interview, and you can even use them to get common ground with the interviewer or decision-maker.

But more about that in chapter 6.

Miscellaneous – professional memberships etc.

There are other sections that might be relevant to your CV. I'll list some here, because as previously mentioned, CVs are of course individual, so take note of the things that are relevant to you!

Professional memberships - if you are a member of any professional bodies list them here. These can really add to your credibility and of course, some industries or jobs require your membership, so make sure you keep up-to-date with it.

Authorships - if you've written anything that's been published like papers or books, then here is the place to mention it. It can be quite powerful to show you are an expert in your field.

Speaking gigs – if you have been a guest speaker or done any other public speaking it can be really great on a CV – it shows confidence, communication skills and that you're an expert in your field.

Industry-relevant positions that show thought leadership – this is something that may not apply to many, but if you are on any round table forums or similar then it can be useful to mention this. It shows you keep up-to-date with changes in your industry as well as being well regarded as a contributor, perhaps even at policy level. It could also include being an admin to a specific group online.

Putting it together – print/proofread/perfect

So, you have written all the sections relevant to you, now what?

Firstly, compile them in a simple and smart template (unless you are sending it direct and know ATS isn't a factor). Avoid anything fancy and no two-column CVs, please.

Ensure the font is the same throughout, ideally 11 or 12 point size, 10 if needed. Don't go lower.

Use bold for headings but don't go crazy with bold and italics.

Choose a modern everyday font like Calibri. Times New Roman, Georgia, Helvetica or Arial etc. Personally, I hate Arial, but personal preference is allowed here. Just avoid anything wacky or unusual, if they don't have the font it will default at the other end or just give a bad impression!

Print it! Allow for white space and ensure margins are reasonable and nothing looks squashed. Printing it out may seem old school but it really helps here. Looking at it on a page will really help you spot inconsistencies with formatting, and you can judge if it is readable.

Proofread it! You may wish to instil some help from a literate friend or relative here (most people have a friend like me who can spot a mistake at twenty paces – it is why I started my business as a proofreader!). Use them and get them to check for mistakes.

Read it yourself, out loud, (or use the Microsoft Word read aloud feature), and look for mistakes, but it is harder to spot your own. I haven't proofread this book by myself, even though I have done plenty for clients!

Perfect it! You want to be really brutal here. Edit that profile down so it has the most impact. Make sure the info next to your skills (if you have used that style), is to the point and includes plenty of keywords relevant to your industry.

Career experience bullets should be full of action words and be clear about your achievements, without excessive jargon.

If you are over two pages look at how much NEEDS to be in there. Older jobs should have minimal, if any, info and most recent roles should be the star.

Get another opinion on the content, ask them if they think the profile sounds like you. Do not be afraid to add personality and be bold with how you describe yourself or your why. Standing out for the right reasons is crucial on a CV.

Now, see the next chapter for what NOT to do in your CV.

ATS – the truth

The first thing I am going to address when talking about your CV and what NOT to do is ATS. Applicant Tracking Systems (ATS) are software designed to help recruiters or employers transfer CV information onto their own system and sift through large volumes of CVs. If set up correctly they can be used to select candidates before a human has to look at the CVs. With high volume recruitment or for large corporations this can be a big time saver.

People freak out about ATS being an anti-CV monster. It is not. There is no need to panic about being ATS compliant as long as you keep your CV simple and smart. I will cover some of the formatting no-nos in this chapter as well as other things to be wary of when writing your CV.

As with all the advice in this book it is borne from my experience and having created hundreds of successful CVs for clients, but if you want to wing it with a fancy CV then by all means go for it. The one thing about CVs, there is no perfect design. If you are going to be sending it direct to a decision-maker or company then you have more freedom with your formatting choices, and if you work in a creative industry then you can, of course, showcase some skills on the CV. BUT if you are applying online in any industry, it is worth bearing in mind that ATS may be a factor in the process.

ATS – what are the tricks?

Well, there aren't any … not really. BUT you can format your CV in a way that means ATS won't be an issue.

The real trick with ATS is to make sure you include keywords from the job description, I cover keywords in chapter 4.

So here is what NOT to do.

Columns – Some ATS can struggle to read them so don't bother. Those fancy, free CV templates online in two columns? Avoid. If you would like to list things, perhaps training courses or skills in two or more columns use tabs to create them.

Graphics or images – photos are NOT necessary on UK or US CVs. So never put one on unless you are going for a modelling contract or similar! But otherwise in the UK they don't want to see what you look like as then you might accuse them of discrimination, and unconscious bias is a thing, unfortunately.

Fancy graphic representations of skills or images such as logos are also unnecessary and best avoided. It can make your file size quite large as well, which ATS won't like.

Text boxes and tables – big fat no here. I think they look a little lazy anyway, but they will also cause mayhem with most set-ups of ATS so just don't use them.

Just put the text on the document, don't separate it into boxes. Don't put info in the headers or footers either.

Font choice – as mentioned in the last chapter you want point size 10 to 12 and use an everyday font, not something fancy or unusual. Your CV should be noticeable for the right reasons, the content and the readability! You have no idea who might read it. If it was someone with a visual impairment and it is an italic font in size 8pt, it could lose you the opportunity. Think about accessibility as well as aesthetics.

PDF or Word Doc – use one of these formats, both are usually perfectly acceptable, but do send it in the format they have requested. Word Docs are easily converted into PDFs (just double-check the formatting doesn't go awry!)

It's a journey, not a life story

Whilst telling some of your story can be powerful, please don't bore them to death. I wrote a CV for a client explaining that he overcame a background of poverty where expectations were that crime was a career option, and this was impactful to the reader.

Every job you ever had, every responsibility you held, and every skill you have gained does not need to be on there. If it is over two pages, there better be a good reason. And if it is over three you will fail to convince me that is justifiable. Streamlining is my forte and writing succinctly on a CV is essential.

Focus on the most recent roles in the last ten years and mostly on the last three to five. Yes, it is helpful to see where you came from, especially if you have worked your way from the ground up in an industry or if you have some diverse experience you can draw on now. But you don't need to list all the jobs you have ever had, not unless this is a specific requirement.

Public sector roles in the UK (governmental in the US) may need to know this but they will ask and length-wise that is then a different ballgame. Ideally, you want to show you have progressed. That you are now doing bigger and better things than when you started and that you followed a path of some kind.

Now don't panic if you didn't and your experience is eclectic, or you are changing careers, you can use that to your advantage by addressing it and stating how it makes you more suitable for the role you are going for.

Bear in mind your seniority as well, you don't need to list every software package you can use if you are managerial level. I have seen directors listing Excel as a skill and this is undermining the seniority of the CV in my opinion. Focus on the skills and experience in line with your level, or the level you want to be.

Keep active

I don't mean take up running (ouch, my knees!), but I mean beware of the words you use. Passive phrases on CVs like 'had responsibility for' are not very effective and are overused.

Try and use active words like full accountability, lead, drove. Show you took action and weren't just there for the ride.

While we are on that subject, let me address an objection I have heard from some of my senior clients here. They feel uncomfortable taking credit for a success their team had as they didn't do it, the team did. Now the fact is they led that team, and no one is going to shout about their success as a leader unless they do.

It is not stealing credit for things by stating the facts of what happened if you were in charge.

Try not to repeat words too often as well. And I mean adjectives like implemented or drove etc. Think of new ways to say things and keep the text readable and alive. If you list a ton of projects with implemented in front of each one, that is dull and boring to read. You don't need to swallow a thesaurus but try to be a little bit original and also natural with how you express yourself. Don't use words you don't understand.

Modesty is for the weak

As I have mentioned above, your CV is the place to shout about yourself. Do not be overly modest or hope the reader will assume things from what you have said. If you are great at what you do, and a project succeeded because of your input, then say so!

I understand it can feel uncomfortable talking about yourself in such a positive manner and there is a fine line between bragging and confidence, however, it is possible to speak confidently without coming across as a dick.

You will need to step outside that comfort zone for a while and look at what an impact you have in the places you work then express it on your CV. Reading feedback from managers, colleagues, clients or even friends can help here. How are you generally perceived by others at work, do they find you approachable, knowledgeable? Because that can really help you think of words to describe yourself.

What you want to avoid is a generic description of the skills for someone who does your job. It needs to sound like YOU.

Are gaps bad?

People get pretty scared about gaps in their CV. Now I don't know when you are reading this, but I am writing it in 2021 when we are still in a partial lockdown due to the pandemic and gaps are appearing on loads of CVs due to increased redundancies and furlough.

Now whether this time affected you or not it is likely that you have a gap somewhere in your career. Maybe time off for travelling or to look after children or a loved one who became ill. Life happens and I believe it shouldn't be something we try to hide on a CV. So, the simple answer is no, gaps are not bad, they are realistic.

Small gaps of a couple of months can probably be ignored, however, you may want to address larger gaps and I would go with honesty. There is usually a positive we can take from any break in our career, whether it was for a good or bad reason. So, if you were out of work and did some volunteering or study or even just took time to take up a new hobby then it is valid to put it in when you outline the gap. The fact is, **you attract the right job culture for you by being honest on your CV.**

Case Study - Culture Fit

Stuart was working in a great company, but they got taken over. The new structure and management were awful, and they started to grind him down. In his management position he was able to influence those around him and do his absolute best, but it was such a toxic environment. When he came to me, he was a bit of a broken spirit, as he had started to believe all corporate jobs are bad news.

We chatted and I reminded him there are better places that are right for him, and that his amazing skills would be appreciated in the right environment. We sorted out his CV and LinkedIn approach and most importantly his mindset. And guess what? He did it. He found the confidence to leave the horrid place (his words) and found a great new position where he is thriving! In his own words:

"You made the whole CV process painless, dare I say enjoyable. I would definitely recommend the hours chat; it certainly helped my thinking on what was important to me. You listened to what was important to me and reflected that back in the CV. What I can say for certainty was the confidence gained through your process and attention you paid to putting together two engaging pieces and your help with my LinkedIn post. From that came some positive approaches and now a job offer. So, a simple thank YOU really, it made me feel that I still had something to offer."

Stuart had all that confidence and skill inside, and he got the new role himself, but he just needed to be reminded and guided into tapping into those reasons of why he goes into work.

If you had time off to be a parent or a carer, my opinion is you should state this proudly on the CV. And this is why. If you apply for a job and they hold it against you that you had time off to look after your children, then what kind of employer will they be long term? What will the policy be when you need time off for a family emergency or need to leave early to pick up a child?

As an aside, with mental health issues I understand that it can be controversial to be open about it and don't feel you need to be. Perhaps, call it a self-development break. As many people who have time off for things like depression get well by taking up a hobby, sport or meditation etc. Don't hide gaps or be afraid to say you needed a career break for something that was important to you, just try and keep it as positive as possible.

The content is the star

The content is the thing we want people to notice, so make it legible and don't concern yourself with fancy colours, borders, logos or pictures.

As mentioned above, ATS dislikes graphics, tables et cetera so stay clear of them but be aware they also detract from the main content of your CV. Using a clear layout with bold underlined headings for each section makes it easier to read and therefore easier to find the information they need to choose you for an interview.

Do not make it a treasure hunt to find your skills and experience. Make your skills the star and ensure that your achievements are easy to find. The overuse of italics should be discouraged and also make sure your font size is between 10 and 12 (I know I said this before but I still see too many CVs with tiny fonts!)

Try and write succinctly, avoiding waffle or large blocks of text. Think about what makes something easy to read for you and get someone you trust to give you an honest view. Come and find me on LinkedIn, I might even give you a free CV review.

Don't overshare

I still see a surprising number of CVs with a date of birth and nationality or even a marital status on them. This is entirely unnecessary in the UK or US.

Due to employment law and discrimination law, this information is not allowed to be asked for. So, if you provide this information, you are putting the employer in a difficult position and basically causing them a headache.

The only personal information we want on the CV is your name, location and some contact details. We do not need a full address as I can't imagine you're expecting a reply by snail mail so an email address and a contact number are more than enough, you may also want to include a link to your LinkedIn profile.

As I've mentioned previously, a photo is also entirely unnecessary and generally speaking unwanted. There are, of course, some types, of role that require a photo, but they will ask for this as part of the application process and so including a photo is perfectly okay in those circumstances. Examples could be private security roles, acting, or modelling contracts. But generally speaking, it shouldn't matter what you look like and can cause unconscious bias so leave the selfies for social media.

It is also not required to give the reason you left each previous role. On public sector CVs or governmental resumes (US) this may be required but these are more likely to be applied for by application form.

Don't rely on a speel cheeker, get a second opinion

I can't tell you the number of times I see a CV with a spelling error in it. Typos happen to everyone so make sure you use the spell checker in Microsoft Word or equivalent, but also get someone else to read it through. We all have an annoying friend who picks up on every mistake, I know because I am that friend!

I'm a trained proofreader but I still had the text checked for this book by someone else as well because it is very hard to pick up your own mistakes. CVs are relatively short documents and therefore there is no real excuse for spelling or grammar mistakes and that is the first impression someone will get of you.

One thing to be aware of are headings, if they are in capitals, anything in capitals will be by default not checked by the Microsoft Word spell checker. You can change this setting, but most people don't remember to. Unfortunately, this means I see a lot of CVs with an error in the heading, something like professional spelt with two Fs. This gives a horrible first impression to someone, who at this point probably doesn't know you in any way apart from your CV.

If you can't pay attention to detail and create an accurate CV, then how will you do a good job for the potential employer? I know having a condition like dyslexia can make it really difficult and being a perfect speller is not essential for the majority of jobs, but using due diligence and asking for help when you need it are skills that will be expected in most roles.

Liar liar

Whilst it may be tempting to claim bigger wins than you achieved or even take credit for things you weren't involved in, I would advise against it. You never know who might see it and you also don't want to get a role based on a blatant lie. Whether you believe in karma or not things do tend to come back to bite you!

Now I'm not going to sit here and tell you never to exaggerate at all but you have to live with whatever you write on the CV. Be aware you may get questioned about anything at interview and you may even have to prove certain things. Claiming you got a first in your degree or made your last company £2 million in sales are pointless lies to make as they can be checked up on.

Blagging things at interview or stating you have a bit more experience than you do because you know full well you can hit the ground running with something is one thing and an out and out lie is another, so just be careful and make sure you can back up whatever is on that CV.

Is there a perfect CV?

Of course not. However, there are some basics you need to get right and if you want to know about structure look at chapter 2.

The most important bit about a CV is it needs to be about YOU. It can be too easy to cut and paste in some clichés about working well in a team and by yourself, or autonomously if you're trying to sound uber professional. But is that really telling a potential employer or recruiter anything about you?

Not really.

Get back to basics and remember who you are and what your offer. Don't be scared to pepper in some personability and be confident. No one else is going to step up and sell you to an employer, you need to do this yourself on your CV.

Think clearly about what it is you want to do (see chapter 1 for help) and then create a CV hitting that goal, showing you as a great candidate and a person worth speaking to further.

Remember the **CV is a foot in the door and is there to get you the interview, not the job.**

Adapt or die

For pity's sake don't send the same CV to every application. Sending the same CV to hundreds of applications is a highly risky strategy. You may get lucky and get a few interviews, but the best approach is to adapt your CV for every role.

I don't mean write a brand new CV every time, that would be insanity, but adapt and tweak the profile and key skills, so it is showcasing how you meet the criteria required. If you have a career highlight you could change it to examples most relevant to the job you are applying for as well.

In some cases, it might be sensible to have a few versions of your CV created. Perhaps if you are aiming for a couple of distinct roles that don't overlap enough or you want one aimed at perm roles and one at contracting.

Having a couple of versions that are clear in their intent can be better than one generic one that doesn't quite cut it.

How to find keywords

This isn't that hard as long as you have a job description or person spec. Even if it is just a job advert, look through and highlight all those keywords that apply to the role.

I am talking about the skills, experience and qualities that are required or desired for the role and then putting those into your CV (as long as you are being truthful).

Here is an example of a job advert and the keywords have been highlighted in bold to show you:

We are a mobile **Ice Cream** event company that have a fleet of Ice Cream vans in Cheam, Sutton area, and we are looking for a **dynamic, reliable, hardworking** member to join our team full time.

Applicants must: -

Be able to speak good **English**

Be trustworthy and reliable

Have great **customer service** skills

Be **well presented and polite**

Have a **full driving licence cat B**.

The role will include: -

Serving ice cream and drinks. **Receiving money** from customers and giving correct change. Keeping the van **clean and tidy** throughout your shift and giving it a thorough clean at the end of each day and before each shift. Keeping the van well stocked.

To be a part of our successful team you don't need any formal qualifications but you must love **working with the public**, be able to work on your **own initiative,** be able to handle cash and you must be **very well organised**. You must also be able to **work under pressure** (there is usually a queue wherever we go!).

This is a great opportunity to work with a growing, successful and popular local business. A uniform and full training is provided.

How to hit the mark

Try to be objective about your CV and think about it from a potential employer's perspective. Would YOU invite yourself for interview? Get someone else's opinion too, someone you trust, but do be careful with asking all and sundry as not everyone is going to give you useful advice here!

The best CVs I have read or written, are not a bore fest. They don't waffle on for pages with little direction or impact. They are interesting, show personality, succinct and to the point and they are EASY to read. It should not be complicated to find out what your skills and experience are, it should be obvious on the first page. Now is not the time to be subtle or hope they assume certain things. If you want them to know you are great with customers and at building rapport, then say so.

Rewording your CV to include keywords from the advert is really important and can give you an edge over others who just haven't bothered.

Be a step ahead of the competition

A great way to give yourself edge is by adding in keywords, as we've said. But you can take this a step further.

Research the company and take a look at their style and tone of voice online and the working culture they project. Bear this in mind when tweaking that CV.

Now, here it gets interesting. As I have harped on about being yourself, so why would I suggest compromising that and matching a company's style. That isn't exactly what I mean. If you are finding yourself having to adapt the CV too much or completely change the way you approach things to fit in with their style, then rethink applying.

For example, perhaps it is a very corporate and formal style and your CV is more outgoing and relaxed with lots of personality. There may be times you want to tone it down, but if you are going to have to redo it so much it doesn't sound like you anymore, just to get an interview, then maybe it wouldn't be the right place to work. The last thing you want is to get a job somewhere you don't feel like you fit in. It is a horrible feeling.

So, bear this in mind and be honest with yourself.

Keep it consistent

Consistency is important, and by that I mean what you say on your CV should be what is also represented on LinkedIn or elsewhere online. With a CV you will tweak it for applications, and you won't want to change LinkedIn every five mins but do make sure the basics are the same such as the job titles and dates. These things are not areas you should be changing anyway, as you should always be honest with where you have worked and when!

Think about the message your CV is portraying of you and make sure LinkedIn is singing from the same hymn sheet. If a hiring manager loves the sound of you on the CV then checks LinkedIn and you have zero personality on your profile or worse still you can be seen to have left arsey comments on people's posts, that is not going to do you any favours.

This is where being true to yourself really pays off, as then it is easier to be consistent across the board.

Don't forget platforms such as Instagram, Twitter and Facebook. It can be policy to check all online presence on social media for recruiters or companies now and you don't want this to ruin your chances. Just remember if you put it online, potentially anyone can see it (excuse me, I am just off to delete my OnlyFans account … hahaha!).

Don't trip yourself up

I have mentioned this already but be truthful!

I don't mean never exaggerate at all or tell the odd white lie about how much experience you have and play the rules 100%, but don't tell big whoppers, you will get caught out.

If you pretend you know some software a little better than you do, and you can learn up on it before you start, that isn't really a lie. If you say you are an Excel expert, but you have never even created a spreadsheet, that is a problem.

Inventing jobs or projects that didn't happen or covering up gaps just isn't cool. And when you get found out you will regret it big time. It can be frustrating when people want a degree you don't have but inventing one for yourself is not the answer.

I believe that actions have consequences, and you may find something you get away with now comes back with a vengeance later on. Plus, you would never be able to relax in a role if you got it under false pretences.

If you claim to have increased sales by 60%, I hope you really did as they may ring someone and ask! Be aware that if you lie to get in they can sack you if they find out.

Think about the audience

With your CV and LinkedIn, it is important to remember you are not writing for you, you are writing for an audience. So, who is that audience?

As a business owner we talk about customer avatars and ideal customers but as a job seeker you need to think from a hiring manager's perspective. They want someone who is reliable and positive and will have a good impact on their business.

How does your CV make you sound? And does it look like you have jumped from role to role for example? Make sure to address this if you have. Perhaps indicate they were contracts or show when a company closed down, for example.

Reason for leaving is not needed on a CV but sometimes it is prudent to mention something if it is through no fault of your own and it has led to a number of roles in a short space of time.

This book is being written in 2021 while a global pandemic rages and lockdowns are still a thing. So, employers are expecting to see gaps on your CV in 2020/21 and I truly believe less stigma will be attached to gaps because of it. But keep it positive and include what you did during a gap. Perhaps volunteer work, training online or childcare. You may have sat around in your pants watching The Tiger King or Friends reruns on Netflix, but don't include that!

Tricks of the trade

Here is where you might want to be a bit sneaky, bearing in mind what I just said about not tripping yourself up! You could try and befriend someone on LinkedIn who already works at a company you are applying to and get some insider knowledge on things. Or perhaps build up some rapport with a recruiter who may then be more inclined to put you forward for roles.

You will know if you are the kind of person who can pull off this type of blag move or if you're not. It isn't right for everyone but sometimes charm and persuasion can give you exactly the edge you need to get the dream job or opportunity.

Perhaps you are going for a role and you know exactly who the hiring manager is. You could do some due diligence and research them online. Find something that you have in common and include it on your CV if you can (this works well with a hobby or interest).

This little trick can sometimes get you a foot in the door and will most certainly open up some great conversations if you get the interview. Humans like people who are interested in the same things, and finding common ground is a powerful tool.

If you like this sort of approach, you will love chapter 6 on finding them and following up!

CHAPTER 5
MAKING LINKEDIN WORK FOR YOU

Why use LinkedIn?

As previously mentioned, there are 756 million users on LinkedIn so being on there is a fast-growing trend and the best way to network professionally with people all over the world.

Most companies are represented in some way on there now and it is one of the best methods to get close to or build a relationship with senior leaders at a company you want to work for.

It is also a place to showcase your personality, thought leadership and skillset.

If you get it right, you can create an engaged and active audience that is relevant to you and opportunities may come your way.

This chapter outlines exactly how to go about using it to its full potential. It is where I have grown my network (21k followers at time of writing) and I have gained a lot of business from it I can tell you.

A kick-ass profile

The most important thing with LinkedIn is to get engagement and drive people to your profile. If you're a business on LinkedIn, obviously you want to use this profile to convert people into leads. However, if you're there to look for a job or build a network to create opportunities, you are looking for a similar effect. You want people to engage with you, and ultimately look at your profile. Or maybe you're applying for roles, and they look you up on LinkedIn, either way your profile needs to kick some ass.

It is a waste of time if you get people to look at your profile, and then there's nothing to read. There are ways to drive people towards your profile which I'll discuss later in the chapter, but you need to have a profile worth looking at.

So, what are we talking about? There are obviously different elements to the profile, and a few things to consider, I will discuss the About section, taglines, banners, photos and skills in the following sections.

The About section

The summary or About section is the main part really, it needs to be a maximum of 2600 characters, so you can't go crazy here, but you should be writing more than one or two paragraphs.

Start off by engaging the reader, tell them something important about you and your skills or experience or that just grabs attention. For business About sections, I will use something that addresses a pain point.

It may or may not be so relevant for a job seeking About section, but it can work if you're saying that you can fix someone's problem in their business and you're going to come in and turn it around, for example.

Talk about the impact you've made. Talk about the skills and experience you've got and where it's from. You can use a fairly informal tone, as it is social media at the end of the day.

I would recommend adding a little bit of personal detail towards the end of the About section, maybe something you do in your spare time or something about your family, whatever you're comfortable sharing or somewhere you like to travel to or just something that's important to you.

With mine I've added that I support the Texans, Liverpool Football Club, and also that I do pole fitness and aerial hoop in my spare time, and I've also mentioned that the reason I'm in business is for my children and their future. It's nice to add those things in because people feel like they get to know you a little bit better. And you may share common interests, the foundation of most relationships.

You should also add some form of call to action. So, for a business it might be 'DM me if you want a free quote', but for a job seeking profile you could have 'If you have any opportunities you feel will suit me, please contact me' and then you can give an email address or a phone number, it's up to you how you want people to contact you. It can be as full of personality as suits you.

If you don't want it to be so outwardly job seeking, obviously some people are in a job at the moment and are looking for something new without wanting to shout about it, you can still say something like, 'I enjoy networking with people in my industry, please feel free to click connect'. It's nice and welcoming, and it gives people something to do after they've read your About section.

Taglines and banners

Now, as part of your kick-ass profile, you will be needing a good banner. The banner is the top part of your profile page, just behind where your photo is at the top. You can create these yourself, or you can get someone to do it for you. There are obviously some great graphic designers that will do lovely LinkedIn banners for you. I recommend Danny Townley who did mine!

This can be costly but worthwhile if you're thinking of keeping the same banner for some time. However, if you're perhaps looking for a new job and thinking of changing again once you get it, it may be a lot of money to pay out to only change it again a month or so later.

This is obviously a personal choice and will depend on your budget, but you can create your own if you use something like Canva. You can search for LinkedIn banner templates. Make sure you resize to use the correct measurements which are 1584 x 396 pxs (at the time of publication). Then you can put anything you like!

The left-hand side will be covered by your photo so try not to put anything important here. You can use a photo behind or background image that relates to you in some way or you could just use some colours or graphics or some simple shapes. Canva will have a few ideas here for you. Have a look at other people's.

Then you need to think about adding some words that relate to your skills or experience and what you're offering. Perhaps a favourite quote or one client has a word cloud about diversity and inclusion, which looks great. You may also wish to add a call to action here of your phone number or an email address, or just 'Feel free to connect'. This will help you gain more connections, as you're encouraging people to connect with you, which is also what you want to do with the tagline.

Taglines - lots of people just use their current job title as a tagline, which is fine, that's what it defaults to on LinkedIn. However, your tagline could say anything you like.

The first forty characters are what people see when you comment on posts. So, these forty characters need to summarise you in some way and give people an inkling of what you're about or what you can do. Personally, for mine (at the time of writing), I have 'My kick-ass CVs get interviews for executives | In-depth CV and LinkedIn help | Proofreading & Editing | Pay It Forward Enterprise | Ice cream fanatic

It shows people exactly what I do. And if someone needs a CV they'll then click through onto my profile and take a read. That's what you want, something that encourages people to click on you and take an interest, so whatever it is, it needs to be clear, or interesting.

You can just have a job title, obviously, and then list skills after it, make use of all the space you've got here. You can have something more interesting, a really funny one that one of my clients uses is 'putting the prod in production'. He then goes on to say that he coaches and supports leaders in production engineering. Obviously, that shows some of his character and personality, that he's a very energetic driven person who will come and turn around a business. It gets across a good message, so try and think about something that works for you.

Photo, skills and the rest

Let's start with the picture. The photo you use should represent you, clearly. Not only is that in the terms and conditions but people will relate to you better if it's a photo of you not a logo or a landscape.

Using anything other than a photo of you does potentially risk getting taken down. So, go for a nice clear face-on photo.

It doesn't need to be a professional headshot, selfies do work or get someone to take a photo of you. Often it works well if you take the background out, there are a few apps to do this. And then just add a standard colour behind, or if you're good at Photoshop, you could always Photoshop yourself in front of something cool, or just do something with a relatively simple background, nothing too cluttered.

In a bar with your friends? Not really the look you want to go for. It doesn't need to be you in a suit, you can wear whatever you like. But let's keep it appropriate. Obviously, if you're a personal trainer then you in workout kit is fine. If you are an MD of a company, perhaps a suit or smart casual look is better, obviously use some common sense here.

There is also a cover story option here that LinkedIn has introduced, where you can add a thirty-second video. It appears when you click on someone's profile photo. To add one yourself, click on the plus sign on your photo and record one or upload one you have pre-recorded. Check mine out for a great example of how to do it! Created by the awesome Nick Raeburn.

For the rest of the profile, you have space for up to fifty skills, so I recommend you put all fifty on there. There are loads of skills to choose from, aim for things that are in your target career. And obviously, be truthful.

Recommendations are like reviews or references that other people write for you. Try and get some from people that know you, people who have worked with you in the past or currently. If you can build up lots of recommendations they work really well.

That's how I get a lot of my clients, because they read my recommendations. I have over sixty-five, however, even if you're looking for work, having some well written recommendations from people that work with you is really strong social proof.

There are other areas to be completed, career experience is self-explanatory, the jobs you've done, the dates you've done them, add some explanation of each one. Use similar to what you have on your CV. You can put as much or as little as you like here, well there's a limit but it's 3000 characters so there's plenty of space. You can add links to projects or add photos as well. It all adds to the keywords when someone is searching for someone with your skills.

Under accomplishments you can add memberships, qualifications/training, and you can add in any voluntary work you've done. You can also mention if you're open to helping people, or connecting or whatever you are open to, and you can add pages or companies you're interested in. It all complements the overall picture you want.

What you're looking for is an all-star profile, and you'll achieve that when you've got everything filled in correctly. The About section is the real core to it though, and everything else should match up with your CV, so make sure the jobs that are on your CV are also on LinkedIn and vice versa.

N.B. There are constant changes on LinkedIn and at the time of writing there are options to use creator mode and add services, I have done both as I am a business. Assuming you are using LinkedIn for work and that is why you are reading this book, don't worry about it too much, or follow my good friend John Esperian on LinkedIn and get all the up-to-date info from him!

Comments versus content

The age-old question of should I be producing lots of content to get engagement or should I just be commenting? Well, the answer is both. But if you have a very small network to start with just posting content will not get you very far. Not many people will see it, especially if you're just starting out. So, focus on commenting!

What you need to do is set aside a period of time every day (or week if time is tight but you get out what you put in), it need only be half an hour, to search out some posts that are relevant to something in your industry or things that you're interested in, or people that you want to connect with, and comment on their posts.

You could search by hashtag for something in your industry that's relevant to you, and then comment on some of those posts you find. If you look for posts that are well received, or people that are already getting good engagement, your comment could get seen by thousands of people. If you make a particularly funny or interesting or insightful comment, it could get liked by hundreds of people, potentially, that's a lot of people you could invite into your network, or at the very least would suddenly find out who you are.

If you start doing this regularly, you build up people who have an interest in you, and who believe that you know what you're talking about. Leaving insightful comments on other people's content from your industry is really helpful. It can also encourage conversation and helps them on their posts so they will value it as well. You can also look for posts under the LinkedIn newsfeed. If you're in the UK use LinkedIn News UK, or you can just use the general LinkedIn news one. I had one for example, that got seven-hundred plus likes and I did get quite a lot of leads from it, and some actual clients, because it got seen by so many people.

Build this into your daily routine to grow your network and increase your engagement. Once you're starting to get far more engagement you can think about posting things. I've said something about what to use for your content later in this chapter. But don't get too stressed about posting, and then not getting much engagement in the beginning, that's normal.

It's a long term game on social media, you're not going to get overnight success. Very few people ever do, I won't say no one because some do. But for most people, it's a case of growing your network slowly, and your engagement will build in time. So, if you're trying to look for opportunities and work, commenting and engaging with the people that are relevant to you and your industry is where you should be focusing your time.

Growing your network

We've talked about growing your network here by engagement, and obviously commenting or posting, and then connecting with people that engage, or that like your posts, or that like your comments, which you can do.

I would suggest that if you want to start growing and sending connections to people the best way of doing this is to look at their profile and engage in some of their posts first before you click the Connect button. If they've already engaged with you then obviously, that's fine. But you also need to think about who you want to grow your network with.

Personally, I accept connection requests from pretty much anyone unless they look super dodgy. People who are Bitcoin investors, or people who have very new accounts that are overly good looking, are usually all scammers, just to be aware of. However, try not to overly pre-judge people as you never quite know who they are or who else they know, even if they're not very relevant to you or your industry, perhaps someone in their network has the best opportunity ever.

What you can do is connect with anyone who asks, and then if they're rubbish or annoying, get rid of them afterwards. And by that I mean just disconnect or block if you have to.

But what you also want to do if you're trying to actively grow your network is find influencers in your industry. Look for people that are creating content. For example, in marketing, look under the hashtag marketing, and some of the other associated hashtags, see who's getting a lot of engagement in those realms. You've got obvious people that have big followings like Gary Vee, but think a bit deeper than that and go for people that are leading in your industry, but perhaps not at the absolute top or who create content you really enjoy. This way, you've got more chance of actually engaging with them and getting them to connect back with you.

A lot of the very big players will have follow first on which means on their profile the main option is to follow, (follow first is becoming more favoured by LinkedIn so more people are doing it), you can still try and connect by clicking the three dots and selecting Connect. This works fine and if you've already engaged with them, they may well accept, however if they've already got their maximum number of connections because there is a limit on LinkedIn, then they're not going to be able to connect with you, you can only follow them, which is still useful in itself, but doesn't really grow your network.

Also think about specific places you might want to work, or if you know you want to work for a charity you could target charities and start to look for people that work at those places and do the same thing.

Look for their posts, engage on them a little bit, so that they get to know who you are, before you click Connect. That way you can build relationships with people, and you're offering them some value by engaging on their posts first, rather than just expecting them to accept a connection request from a random person.

Mix business with pleasure

Here are some content ideas, they are not specific ideas, but I would like to give you some subject areas or content types that work really well.

Firstly, rants. Everyone loves a good rant. These always seem to get good engagement or work well partly because they're so passionate, it can be quite tongue in cheek, of course, it could be about pineapple on pizza, or your hatred for some TV programme or something quite innocuous, or it could be a proper rant about the bad service you've received from a company (obviously make sure in that case, that it's factual). But a good rant about something, either petty or something important to you, can work really well, and be really, really funny.

Educational posts. Sharing value is really important. It shows that you are knowledgeable, an expert in your subject and your industry. Sharing information and facts, for example I share CV tips quite regularly, can really help other people. Sharing educational things, or whatever you know about and what your skill set covers can help to build up your reputation as an expert in your field or a thought leader, or at the very least someone interesting to connect with.

Funny, entertaining posts. Everyone loves a good meme. As long as it's appropriate, sharing a meme or sharing a funny thing you found on the internet, or a funny story, or a terrible joke all work. As long as these things are true to you and broadly appropriate, then go for it. Funny stories with children or things like that, often work really well. Fridays are often a good time to share something funny, but obviously that's up to you. There are some lines you shouldn't cross though and remember potential employers are watching.

Vulnerable. Sharing something vulnerable or a personal story to you, or any other kind of personal post can work really well. If you're comfortable with it, sharing for example a photo of your child on their birthday or something that they've achieved or done.

Personally I have shared about my journey of discovering my daughter is autistic, through the assessment process. That's something that's really opened up a lot of new connections for me. It's something that's really important to me. And it's also got me some new clients, funnily enough, because when you are open about something that's so big and important in your life other people can really relate to it. If you are a parent and post about a child not sleeping, other parents will relate to that, and sympathise with you. And that is how you build meaningful connections.

Be yourself

So here we talk about really being yourself, it's not rocket science, although some people find it very difficult being authentic. This word is horribly overused now, but it's really important. Bring out that human voice in your content. And by content, I mean comments as well. It's important because people get to know the real you.

Don't worry about having some online persona. Just be yourself. Although obviously I don't encourage too much swearing or things that will break the LinkedIn rules, but that should go without saying. Personally I love swearing but LinkedIn doesn't!

By being yourself, I mean saying what you think. When you're talking about your work or yourself, or commenting on someone's posts make sure it's something you actually mean, or that you actually think. Don't say things because you think it's what people want to hear.

Being real is something humans look for. We'll search for it, especially online, we also notice when people aren't real. We all have that instinct. Most people can tell when a post is bullshit. So, stick to real life, stick to real things that mean something to you, and stick to being yourself. At the end of the day the person you are online should be who you are in real life so if we meet you in the street it will be the same person.

This goes for the kind of images you share like selfies. Using too many filters etc. is inadvisable because it's just not the real you, is it? Obviously, that's a personal choice. But being yourself will work. It feels weird sometimes, especially at the beginning, and it can feel a bit vulnerable, but if you've got an opinion on something and you stand for something, then make that clear.

Don't be scared, because the worst thing that can happen is some people don't like it. And you know what those people were never going to like you anyway. And who cares, you don't want all those people to like you, you think differently to them. Your vibe attracts your tribe. It's a bit of a cliché saying now, but it's true. And what you want to build on LinkedIn is an engaged network of people that you get on with, and that get you. So, by being yourself, that's exactly what you will do.

Be brave

By being yourself and being a bit brave with the things you say you will find you will gather some really strong connections with people, and you can build a really good network of people who actually care. Standing up for things you believe in is really important. Also, being brave with things like video works really well because most people don't do it.

Out of the 756 million users on LinkedIn, only 1% actually create content, even less of those people create video. So, if you're brave enough to do a video you will stand out. Keep them short by the way, the limit is ten minutes but I would stick to about ninety seconds if you've never done one before. And try and put captions on if you can, places like rev.com will do it for you for a small fee or find an app - Apple users have Apple Clips and there's Autocap for both Android and Apple. Lots of people watch videos without the sound on and it also means your videos are accessible to people with hearing impairments.

Using video can help you really stand out and it also helps people get to know you.

If you are brave enough to be vulnerable it will pay off. What I mean by being vulnerable is sharing a story of something that's happened to you. Mental health is quite a big one here that works really well for people because you're sharing it and talking about it in an open way that will help other people who can share their stories too. It will also help people understand you are who you are. It's a part of you and shows you've overcome something.

Keep it positive

Following on from being brave, it's all very well being yourself or being vulnerable, but let's not make every post negative or about something terrible that has happened. Keep it to things that you've overcome.

Talk about a challenge you've been through, maybe a period of time where something bad happened, or you came out the other side. How did you get through it? I've done a story on LinkedIn about how I was homeless, years ago. That is obviously a story of how I came through that and how I am where I am now, and it's a part of my journey.

Obviously, bear in mind that if you are looking for future employers, posting constantly about how depressed you are is not going to attract them. But frankly it's not going to attract anyone and if you're constantly posting negative vibes, you're going to get negative vibes back. So, think about that, be mindful about how and when you share vulnerable posts.

Embrace your weird/uniqueness

We are all unique and like I have said many times in this book being yourself is essential, but you know those little weird things you do, or quirky parts of you that make you you, imagine sharing those.

It can feel scary as we have said with being vulnerable, but showing the real you, weirdness and all (within limits!) can really help you become a. more human and b. more relatable. Very few weird habits/likes are totally unique so imagine finding someone else who likes Weetabix with butter (yes, I do eat that!).

I also find that sharing something like a weird food combo or an unpopular opinion can be really funny and engaging as a post. By the way, I hate cheese and musicals, but it doesn't make me a bad person. Weird? Yes!

Whilst you want to gather an engaged network of people that may create opportunities in the industry you are aiming to get a job in, it is also great to build up a supportive and fun network at the same time.

As long as you set some reasonable parameters of what is socially acceptable then don't be afraid to show your quirky or geeky ways.

They are watching you

Don't ever forget that everything you post online, every comment you make, every like you click, leaves a trail, and anyone can see that.

If you're liking an inappropriate post or you're joining in with a conversation, something that might be seen as negative in your industry or joining in a political or racist debate, anything that would put you in a poor light, stay away.

I don't mean don't stand up for people. I mean don't do the opposite. Don't bully people, don't troll people, don't leave nasty comments, don't get into really silly arguments. Don't be overly negative, because people are watching.

You might not realise it, they might not like your posts, they might not comment on them, they might not even be an active connection or follower, but people can see it. And when your profile gets looked at by a potential employer because they've got your CV, or they're just looking for someone with your skills, they might have a quick look at all your engagement, and obviously this could count for any other social media platform as well. And they can see exactly what you've been doing.

Remember it's not just about what you're posting, what you like or engage with in any way will still be seen. So, make sure this puts you in the best possible light, not the worst.

Sometimes, it can be good to have a quick look through your engagement and activity on the profile, just to double check what someone else would see if they looked at it. Would they see someone who is a positive, happy person, engaging with interesting posts, and giving value or being funny? Or would they see a negative Nigel or Nina?

It must also be said that lurkers in themselves are not a bad thing, that is what we call the people who never engage on your posts but watch everything, maybe they really like you. There might be people following everything you write, and they think you're great, they just don't always tell you. As a business owner, those people often turn into clients. So I always have to be aware that even posts that don't seem to do that well, may gather me leads. Because the people who are interested will message me privately. Now, this could still apply to job seeking and building a network because someone could be watching what you're doing, picking up on everything and then when an opportunity comes up in their business or with someone that they know they'll put it your way because they already know who you are and what you're about.

So even when posts, or comments don't do well, just remember, you never actually know who has seen them. Never underestimate it. But for goodness' sake go back and delete anything that shouldn't be there on your timeline right now!

Jobseeker must-haves

It sounds super obvious, but don't forget that there are loads of jobs listed on LinkedIn.

There are some LinkedIn specific functions for job seeking, and you can apply for jobs direct on LinkedIn. It will match your key skills with roles that come up and show you roles to apply for as well, but do be aware the competition is rife as is it so easy to apply.

Use the search function and subscribe to job alerts or keep an eye on status updates to follow new listings before they're advertised. You can also check out internships and graduate jobs on the LinkedIn student portal. Follow companies you'd like to work with so you're first to know about any job opportunities, graduate schemes or expansion plans. And as mentioned elsewhere, connecting with people who work at places you are interested in can be a great way to get the inside track.

There is an option to show you are open to work on LinkedIn, and it creates a green ring around your profile photo. Go to Settings> Jobseekers preferences> Let recruiters know you're open to work> Change to yes & click learn more> Enter job titles- (Up to 5)> Add locations- (Up to 5)> Amended Start date- (Immediately, I'm actively applying/ Flexible, I'm casually browsing)> Select Job Types- (Full-time, Contract, Part-time, Internships, Temporary, Remote)> Choose who sees you're open to work> Add open to work hashtag & green frame to your profile.

There are two schools of thought with this. It can be useful as then you will be targeted with opportunities by recruiters, but that in itself can be a pain as not every recruiter has your best interests at heart, and you may get bombarded with pointless enquiries. It can also be viewed by some as a bit desperate, but I would say the majority of people don't think like that so use your own personal choice here. Obviously, if you are looking for work whilst still working elsewhere you won't want to do anything so obvious anyway.

There are two relevant hashtags to be aware of: #Opentowork and #Offeringhelp. By searching #Offeringhelp you will be able to find individuals who are offering FREE services to assist you including: CV reviews, mentoring and so much more! For example, I offer free CV feedback to people ... my hashtag is #KickassCVs - give it a follow!

If you go into settings and find JOB APPLICATION SETTINGS, this will allow you to upload your CV in DOC, DOCX or PDF Format. Once you have updated your CV, upload it here. You can then select 'Quick Apply' when searching through jobs, which saves you time in uploading or sending your CV individually for each application. HOWEVER, I would very much advise you to tweak your CV for every application, so I don't really advocate this approach, but I didn't want to leave it out as it is an option on offer.

CHAPTER 6
FIND THEM AND FOLLOW UP

Fortune favours the brave

Playing it safe will only ever get you so far, and this chapter is about pushing things a little bit further than perhaps your average person would. If you can even apply just a couple of the things you might give yourself enough edge to stand out above the rest.

Firstly, it will require some bravery and the ability to let go of shame. Now I am not suggesting we are sending naked photos to people, that definitely isn't the approach I would suggest (although I am sure in some instances it would work, but let's not go there!)

What I mean is remember that life is short, people don't care about you and what you do as much as you do and that stepping outside your comfort zone and letting go of the fear of looking silly is a powerful tool.

How is this relevant to you in this context?

Well, it is, because if you stick your head above the parapet, it might get shot off. And standing out online or to potential employers may mean some people don't like it or friends mock you.

Take posting videos online as an example. You may start to include video in your content on LinkedIn and I can bet you some old workmates will try and rib you about this. Or family may mock you or misunderstand. Don't let this put you off. Just let go of the pride a little and go for it.

What ARE the rules?

Where we're going, we don't need rules! Oh okay, maybe there are some. But when it comes to job-seeking and networking and putting yourself out there the rules are common sense.

Don't do anything illegal, highly offensive or that can come back and bite you too hard. Being a bit daring by calling a CEO or sending a gift to a decision-maker (more on that later) is one thing, sitting outside an office building and following people home is quite another (that is called stalking and I haven't done it since I was about ten, not sure that counts).

Don't do things that will aggravate or offend and whilst controversial posts may gain engagement on social media, always consider how that will affect people's view of you. If you are controversial without purpose it could paint you as an angry type who stirs up trouble, and let's face it, not very employable. So just be MINDFUL when you post online or when interacting with people.

Persistence not pestilence

Following up with people or tracking down decision-makers can have a great effect. However, don't overdo it! No means no so if people don't reply, don't bombard them or become a nuisance.

That being said, some persistence may be required to get where you want to go. So if that means sending a few messages and posting some mail, or finding email addresses and using them, you need to stick at it. But use common sense and instinct and if someone seems to be getting annoyed then leave it alone.

Pestering a recruiter for example can pay off, but don't go too far. Do things in a fun and friendly way and they won't mind. They will then enjoy their interactions with you and are more likely to go the extra mile or put in that good word. Most of us can sense when we are being an unreasonable dick about it, but if you don't have the sensor, probably best not to try this approach at all.

Case Study
Persistence Pays Off

Esther wanted to work in marketing and try as she might she was not getting the interviews with her CV. She in fact won a free CV from me so we worked on getting it up to scratch. With a more focused approach and making sure her passion for marketing was at the forefront, the new CV was ready.

The job market in 2020 was tricky, as most people know, but persistence paid off and I got this message a few months later:
"Finally got a marketing job!!! Your CV format definitely helped; I would like to write a review!

Which read as so:
"Rebecca is the CV expert I was looking for, I had a strong experience background but with a competitive arena in my area plus the pandemic around, Rebecca helped me to make my CV a stronger one and more attractive. I had more interviews than before and got a new job too! Highly recommended plus she is so nice and funny!"

She has also now got a role in the public sector, which was the ultimate dream, so it really paid to be patient and persistent and keep trying in this case!

Keep it real

Whichever approaches you decide on make sure they feel right to you. It is no good forcing yourself into doing things that are completely against the grain. Pushing out of your comfort zone is good, acting wildly out of character is not. This goes for your LinkedIn interaction and your CV.

You don't HAVE to be outgoing and full of charisma if that isn't your natural character. Introverts are just as valuable, just bear in mind you may need to push yourself a little more than usual if you want to get noticed.

Sharing your real thoughts and ideas and experiences can be so powerful. People don't just buy from (or hire) people, they buy from and hire people they like! So, talking about things you like and thoughts you have will help people get to know you. Then they may like you and trust you!

That know, like and trust trio are well known in marketing for business, but it applies when you are marketing yourself for a new role. In fact, personal branding is really what we are talking about in a lot of this book. Knowing who you are and then getting that across in the best possible way to find the right role for you.

Do you have to keep it formal?

No. Professional yes, but formal no. But be appropriate.

If you are applying to a very formal style of company and that is what you want, then you need to act in that way and present yourself online and in your CV in a formal manner.

If you really want to work in a laidback and more casual environment, then acting and presenting yourself in that way is perfectly acceptable. The CV can be full of personality and the

LinkedIn profile can be the same, plus you can post more laidback and fun posts and interact in a less formal way.

Gone are the days of LinkedIn only being for the professional stuffed white shirts, now it is a relaxed social media platform for the most part, where business and job hunting goes on, but different styles are accepted.

It is becoming more inclusive and diverse as time goes on, thank goodness! I have posted about pole dancing, aerial hoop, ice cream, rock pooling, trees … you name it!

Creative ways to capture attention

The world is your oyster with this one, how creative can you be? There are all sorts of ways to grab attention. I heard of someone posting a mannequin's arm to a potential employer with a note saying I would give my right arm to work here. It got them an interview!

It could be as simple as sending the recruiter who you want to use their favourite flowers or sending muffins to someone to thank them after an interview. There are so many creative ways to get attention in a positive way, much more original than flowers or muffins as well.

If you have your sights on a particular company then you can find out who the hiring manager is or the manager of a department you want to work in, or the CEO (depends on your level and the size of the firm) and perhaps send them a gift you know they will like.

Research online can help you find out quite a lot about people usually. As long as you avoid anything creepy like underwear, it should get you noticed in a good way.

Risky? A little, but it will show a level of effort that most people just won't put in!

The dark art of persuasion

You don't get anywhere in life without learning how to persuade and negotiate. If you are a parent this is probably a daily occurrence. Once you have persuaded a four-year-old to put shoes on, persuading an MD to give you a shot at an interview for a FD role will be a walk in the park!

I remember one interview I went to, and I had no REAL experience or qualifications for it. It was a telesales role at a newspaper and I had done some door to door sales but that was only for a couple of months (it is fun in the summer but when it starts to rain every day, not so much!) Anyway, I got the heads up at the first interview as we got on so well, that the director conducting the second was a real ballbreaker and that she loved confident and straight-talking people. Thankfully that is what I am like although I usually tone it down in interview situations a tad.

Well, I took it head-on and stated I would be great for the role and that I was a chance she should take as I could guarantee I would succeed for her. I got the job, and I was regularly the top salesperson, so I wasn't wrong. But had I been timid or not known her love of the direct approach, I may not have got that opportunity.

This shows the power that knowledge can have in a situation. Giving yourself that edge sometimes is needed, especially if you are trying to break into a new career or an industry you don't have much experience of. So get building rapport with the right people then use every scrap of intel you can get!

It is also a new and innovative idea to get video references! If you can find some people who will give you a great recommendation and record it on video it will be gold. Posting this on LinkedIn or even sending it as part of an application will give you more edge than a dodecahedron!

Risk vs reward

Weigh it up. For the most part, being bold or standing out will not risk that much except maybe some dignity or pride if they don't like it. But imagine the insane reward if you get that opportunity and end up in your dream job/career. Now isn't that worth some risk?

In the great scheme of things we are not talking life-threatening risks here either are we. I am not expecting anyone to try and do a Spider-man style free climb up the company building to get attention. Or a bungee jump off the roof. We are talking about exiting the comfort zone and using your personality and creativity to get yourself a chance.

We tend to regret chances we didn't take, not ones we did. So, think about that when you are freaking out about making a call or sending a gift or talking yourself up in an interview. You need to take some risks in life to get where you REALLY want to go.

The best things don't come easily. Only you have the power to make the changes and put the work in, so go for it.

The power of rapport

Building rapport is an awesome life skill to have as it can help you in multiple situations. Many of us have the natural ability to befriend complete strangers and be chatting away like old friends after a few minutes. I have always been a bit like this and have made friends in the strangest places.

I do think you can learn it as a skill if it isn't your forte though. The key is finding common ground. In the UK, talking about the weather or a long queue works as people always have an opinion on them. If you are both parents that works or if you can find another shared interest. Even professional relationships are far stronger when you find something in common that you can chat about. Music, football teams, gaming, travel, children, culture … the list is endless.

And we are spoilt now with social media as it is much easier to find things out about people in advance. But even if you can't, you can still find something just by asking a few questions or more importantly by listening to things they say.

In person, mirroring body language and listening are two of the key components to building rapport plus eye contact, but don't turn it into a staring match.

Where are the decision-makers?

Most of them are on LinkedIn! Not all might be active but with 756 million users you can guarantee most businesspeople have an account these days. Finding a company is easy enough then it will show you who works there. It will, of course, depend on the set up and hierarchy as to who might be a decision-maker.

Use some detective work here and get hold of as much info as you can. Company websites often list staff and their roles, then you can track them down on LinkedIn. Emails can be worked out if you know their name and the format a company email address takes. I tracked down a client's work email in this way once when I was chasing a bill (which he subsequently paid).

You could connect with someone else who works there and build a relationship with them and find out who is doing the hiring. (By relationship I mean a friendship not anything romantic, I wouldn't take things that far if I was you …!)

Once you know who you need to speak to then you can decide what the best approach is.

CHAPTER 7
YOU DON'T NEED TO ASK PERMISSION FROM ANYONE (BUT GIVE IT TO YOURSELF)

Stop making excuses

You may have considered a career change or shift in job before and never quite done it. Maybe the kids were young, you just moved house, your partner was focusing on their career, all valid reasons. However, at some point you need to put yourself first and this may mean some sacrifices for a short time, but you only get one life (allegedly) and you don't want to waste too much of it not doing what you really want to!

Kids require a lot of attention, and they need you, I have young children and one of them is neurodiverse, I do get it. However, I still make time for my business and my friends and my hobby as that makes me a happier person and therefore a better parent. Do not use your children as an excuse, as one day they will leave home and if you sacrifice it all for them there will be nothing left for you at the end of it. And that is just the brutal truth for some parents.

Retaining a sense of self and doing things you want to do is not selfish, it is necessary in my opinion. Yes, we compromise for our partners in some areas and yes, we change when we have children, but don't lose yourself completely and don't forget about your needs on the way.

You are not stuck

It can't feel like you are stuck for some of the reasons above, which may be excuses or circumstances, but often the truth is we're only getting in our own way.

There is light at the end of the tunnel, people do change careers at any age. Mothers do it, fathers do it, grandfathers do it, grandmothers do it, anyone can achieve a career change if they really want to, unless we're talking about extreme circumstances which, of course, may prevent it but I'm guessing you're not in one of those or you wouldn't have picked up this book.

Once you have a clear aim for your career, a kick-ass CV that showcases your skills and achievements, and the right mindset, then you can get the job you want. Trust me, I've seen it happen multiple times with my clients. Do I help them along the way? Of course I do, but the glory belongs to them. At the end of the day they took the action, they made the changes, and they then nailed their interviews to get the roles they wanted.

Is there hard work along the way for you? Yes, there is. Can you do it? Yes, you can (sorry that does sound a bit like Bob the Builder).

Be one of the 15%

In a Gallup survey, only 15% of workers worldwide said they enjoyed their work. Only 15% ... so 85% of people don't enjoy their job. Just let that sink in. Scary, isn't it?

The thing is you spend quite a lot of time at work, don't you? If you work the standard forty-hour week over fifty years (most of us won't be retiring before seventy without good planning), then that is 104,000 hours … Sure you'll get some time off for holidays, but you'll also work late sometimes and some people work significantly longer than forty hours a week.

Do you want to spend 104,000 hours doing something you dislike, don't feel good about or that doesn't fulfil you on some level? I think the answer is always going to be no.

Now I could be accused of being idealistic here, I appreciate we all have different needs and pressures on us and working whatever job you can find is sometimes the only thing you can do. I have been there. I have done the temping in thankless jobs, being treated like crap and paid a pittance as I did it to survive at the time. Sometimes you do what you have to do. But we are talking about making a plan to get into a role you really want, and if you picked up this book and read this far, I am guessing that is what you want to do.

So don't settle, don't convince yourself it will get better or live for weekends, work to get into a job you really want, take some action!

Everything is a choice

Here is a little reminder that EVERYTHING (apart from, as my husband pointed out, death) is a choice. Now what I mean by this is you may feel you HAVE to live where you do as it is close to an ageing parent, for example. But that is a CHOICE. You may feel obligated to make it, but you choose to stay and look after them or support them from love, or maybe responsibility. But make sure you are aware that you can choose.

This is not me saying abandon people or run away from your family because you can, but I am just reminding you that you should be where you are, doing what you're doing because you have chosen to. Not through some misplaced loyalty or obligation.

Realising this is actually quite freeing. I could pack up and take off to Greece tomorrow if I wanted to. I choose not to as I want to stay and be with my children growing up, but the fact that I could leave helps me to stop feeling trapped.

Maybe that sounds a bit ridiculous … but my brain is a bit weird, we already established that.

The feeling of being trapped can hold you back. **Remembering that every choice you made is how you got where you are can empower you to make better choices to get where you want to go.**

The power of permission

Nobody gets to tell me what to do, that's why I work for myself to be honest (just ask my business coach Dan, I can be a nightmare!) So, I DO NOT mean you need to ask permission from anyone to do what you want to do. You don't. But you do need to give permission to yourself!

This can sound a bit naff (do people still say that?), but if you are anything like me then sometimes you really get in your own way.

We are allowed to be happy though! Life doesn't HAVE to be a slog. You are allowed to dream!

You don't need my permission to do this, but if it helps, you have it, give yourself permission to really go for it. Commit. Go all in. You have probably been half-arsing it or ignoring that nagging voice in your brain for ages, when really you know you need to step up and take some control of your life.

Now is not the time to look back and regret you didn't do it sooner, now is the time to start.

And congratulations, because you have already started!! Just reading this book will get you off to a flyer.

What does it FEEL like in the wrong job?

What greater motivator than remembering how crap a bad job feels. Even if your role is okay, but not quite lighting that fire. The thought of doing it for, what did we say, 104,000 hours might just tip you over the edge.

Just imagine doing that same commute, or slide from bed to desk, every day for the next however many years. Maybe seeing others come and go. Move on, move up. Make changes and find success. While you just stay static. Probably through indecision or fear. Not good, is it?

Perhaps the boss is a nightmare and belittles you day in, day out. That grinds you down. The confidence ebbs away and you suddenly feel like you can't ever do better. I saw many people get promoted above me in roles as I was always trouble for management. Too much mouth, too sassy and they couldn't handle it. Clients always loved me, and managers said I had an attitude problem.

The fact is I did have an attitude problem but that was because I was never in the right job for me. I lacked motivation, had too many sick days and changed career numerous times. Yet, now I have no one telling me what to do and how many hours to work. So I could slack off all the time, but I work harder than ever when I need to, as it is my choice. Even in a good job the drudgery can get you down, especially if you are not fulfilling your full potential.

What will it FEEL like in the right job?

Let's take it back to positive again now, what about in the right job? How will you feel then? Imagine wanting to go into work every day, feeling fulfilled, like you are making a difference in some way whether for others or yourself and actually feeling like you belong.

No Sunday night dread. No worry that you are going to look back after decades wishing you had changed sooner. No commute of doom. No temptation to take yet another day off sick (I have been there!).

I used to fantasize about finding a dead body on the way to work so it would give me a day off, how messed up is that? I would peer into bushes hoping that my day would be taken over by police interviews and time off for trauma … what a weirdo.

I also imagined being hit by a car, nothing major, maybe just a busted ankle so I could get a few weeks off! That is how much I didn't want to go into work sometimes! You may or may not be quite this bad, but imagine Mondays being the best day and the satisfaction you feel after a great day doing something you enjoy.

You will not have a perfect job as it doesn't really exist (even chocolate tasters have bad days I am sure …) but you will have, on average, far more good days, and the general overall good feelings you get when you are enjoying life.

Work is a huge chunk of your life, you don't have to be somewhere you hate, there is a way out.

Finding your roadblocks

We talked about making excuses and those that may try to tell you you can't do it. But what about if it is you that is telling yourself you are not good enough. If you feel like you have some internal roadblocks in the way, read on.

We need to dig a bit deeper here and it isn't always that comfortable. It might be cliché, but you may need to think back to childhood. Were you told you were not good at something or perhaps struggled at school?

These kinds of early experiences can really affect us.

I will give you an example. I am really academic, did well at school, except with sport. I am naturally short and small so I couldn't do any of it and hated running. Therefore, I grew up with the belief I would never be able to do any sport, so I never really tried. Skip to my fortieth birthday and my friend arranged a pole dancing party. Great fun!

Well, I decided to take pole fitness lessons every week and three years on, no thanks to the lockdowns of 2020, I am still loving it. I have done two photoshoots, a solo performance in a show and am stronger and fitter than I have ever been. I have just started aerial hoop as well, in fact! Because it turns out I CAN do a sport after all!!!

Now that may sound like a strange example, and I am annoyingly proud of my hobby, but childhood experiences and beliefs are the basis of your core self-belief and self-esteem. It all stems from there, so rooting around and delving deep to really look at those beliefs you have about yourself and questioning them, is really important.

It can be powerful stuff! And of course, fully qualified therapists are there to guide you if needed. But just thinking about it all and considering where any confidence issues or self-doubt may be coming from can be enough to help you realise where issues lie. And which beliefs you may need to question or let go of.

You ARE good enough, you CAN do it, and don't let anyone tell you otherwise.

Freeeeeeeeeeeeedom

People often strive for more money and things but what is it you really want? For most of us, it is freedom!

More money can bring that for you as it gives you more choices. But money isn't everything, of course. Moving into a better paid career may be able to give you more freedom, but also there is the freedom to choose your future as we have already touched on.

It is amazing how freeing it can be to work towards the career you really want. Perhaps it is simply that you feel free of your past and full of hope for the future. But I have seen it in clients, and it is like a weight has been lifted. That point when they commit to going for a new role and making a change. It isn't even at the point you get the role, it is deciding to go for it that has the effect.

Making a big decision can often bring a real sense of peace as well and even if you might be having to work much harder for a while just to get into a new career or take a step up from where you are now, the decision to start will bring you mental freedom!

There is also freedom when you are certain about your path and being really honest about what you want, with both others and yourself. Maybe you are a doctor who worked for years and years to get where you are, it can be a gruelling journey. But now you are there, it isn't what you hoped or imagined. Only YOU can decide to change. And if you do, that is not a failure. There is much more likelihood of you feeling regret if you stay put and look back at your career as an old person and wish you had gone to live your ideal life instead of following the plan you set when you were a different person.

We evolve and change as we get older and that freedom of choice that we have can be forgotten, but trust me, you always have it even when you feel like you don't.

Mindset – where is yours at?

Mindset is almost becoming overused as a word (it is right up there with authentic), but it really just means the way your mind approaches something. The way our mind is *set* towards that thing. And in this case, try and be as honest with yourself as possible.

If you are going to make changes and drive yourself into a new role you need to make sure you have your ducks in a row and mindset is going to be a key part of this. Knowing where your mind is at and regularly checking in with yourself is important as a day-to-day thing anyway.

Looking after yourself, and having time for relaxation, self-care, time with loved ones and time away from your normal environment are all really important for your mental health. And your mindset and mental health are interwoven together.

If you are feeling negative or burnt out or just plain meh about life, then that can start to have an effect on your mental health and can become a downward spiral.

I am not here to preach about this as any kind of expert on mental health, but I can tell you from experience that it is precious and we need to maintain it. Don't expect to have a positive, go-getter mindset if you're not looking after yourself mentally and physically every day.

So, go for walks, listen to music, read, take baths, have spa days, eat healthily, go out with friends, whatever it is YOU need to do. It can be tempting to reach for temporary mindset fixers such as alcohol, drugs or indulgent foods, but long term we all know they are bad news.

For me, I have my sport and it keeps me sane! Going to classes not only builds fitness and strength so is physically good for me, it also means I can socialise, and I have to focus on the moves so much that it allows my brain to relax from worry while I am there. The drive there and back is even part of that. As a busy mum of two, time away and without the cries of mumumumumum are welcome and important!

Finding your thing will definitely help your overall mindset. It could just be making time for walking by yourself or with a friend regularly. Or taking the long route home from somewhere. Just build it into your everyday life and do not put maintaining health, mental and physical, at the bottom of the list.

We all need mental resilience and changing career paths will bring a level of pressure you didn't have before, so get yourself in the best possible position and you stand a much better chance of sticking to your plan.

How to ignore the haters

Not everyone will be in your corner and on your side. In fact, if you make a big change or change career or step up, you may find some people really don't like it at all.

Often it is jealousy as they are too scared to do it themselves, sometimes it is fear as they are scared you will change and move on without them. In some cases, you might! We all grow apart from some friends as we mature, and our lives take different paths. Some people stick around for it all and some don't. And that is okay.

Just remember you are doing this for yourself, no one else. And you don't need to justify your actions or indeed explain them. Definitely don't apologise.

Focus on your plan and then stick to it. Not doing something because of what Karen on Facebook said is a terrible idea, which you will regret. Going for your dreams and working hard to get where you want to be you won't regret.

You are the one who has to live your life, so don't let any negative comments about future plans get into your head. Run your own race. Let the haters hate.

I fully appreciate it is not always so easy! But think about how you are going to react and then stick to it. Ignoring the comments is one option, replying with a funny answer or a scathing one is another, or just block them out and focus on the ones who are supporting you. Cutting people out isn't always easy, but like with social media we all need to prune our friends list once in a while and don't be afraid to do this in your life.

I know when it is family or a long-term friend it may not come easy and please don't block your mum's number then blame me, haha. But do think seriously about how much value some relationships are bringing you. Is it even effort wise, do they ever show support or love to you, are they bringing you negative energy? Not always easy questions but important ones.

And sometimes it might even be a family member you decide to speak to less, but either mend a broken relationship or let go of it. Don't soldier on if that person is dragging you down. I don't mean a blip when someone needs help or support, no one is perfect, but I mean a long-term energy vampire, we all know them! The relief is immense when you get the strength to let those people go.

CHAPTER 8
FEEL THE FEAR AND DO IT ANYWAY

What to do about rejections

Reality time, you likely won't get a job of your dreams straight away. Actually, you might, I have genuinely seen this happen with clients when they have their CV and mindset sorted, but in most instances it will take some time.

Making up your mind is half the battle, getting your CV sorted is another key element, but the tenacity and drive to carry on when it goes a bit crap is what you really need to get you over the finish line!

You will get rejected. Job seeking is brutal at times. You might not even get rejections, you might get ignored. You might get an interview with a big opportunity then not get it.

It WILL hurt. But it won't kill you.

In job seeking, every no gets you closer to a yes. And every failed interview is a tool for learning! So, take every rejection as an opportunity to learn what went wrong and work out what you can do to change it for next time. Give yourself time to bitch and moan and throw a big old pity party to get it out your system, then slap yourself with a wet fish and crack on again!

Time to vent is important but try not to let that last too long. Twenty-four hours is plenty I think, and make sure you reset for the next opportunity. Carrying over resentment and bitterness for chances lost will not help you move forward.

Sometimes it is just bad luck, when they prefer someone else or went with more experience (I've had that happen before now). This can be extremely frustrating but don't let it deter you from trying again as the right place for you will take a chance on you. When you are changing career or pushing yourself into a step-up, it may mean you are asking them to really believe in you. So work on being convincing and (don't shoot me for the word usage) authentic.

How to stay positive

Staying positive is key and as I have just said, allow the negative feelings to come out, don't override them or block them as this will cause you problems.

Toxic positivity, which we can sometimes see online these days, whereby you just say everything is great all the time whether it is or not, isn't the answer. Having a positive mindset means accepting shit happens and you can get through it and move on. Vent it all out, however works for you, then get back to the task in hand, which is finding a job.

Making sure you prepare is a great way to stay positive as you will feel more relaxed and less stressed out. Amending your CV before applications (see chapter 4) and prepping for interviews are both key. As is following a great self-care routine like we mentioned in chapter 7.

When it comes to interviews, practise makes perfect and if you are really rusty get someone to set up a mock interview for you. I do this for my clients as I have someone on my team who has interviewed hundreds of people over the years, and it is perfect as you may feel a bit nervous, but it gives you a chance to get helpful and constructive feedback without a job being on the line!

Reminding yourself of your why is crucial when staying positive. I have to do this with my business at times. Staying up late or working weekends like I have when writing this book, can sometimes make me grumble and regret working for myself, but I remember I am doing it to provide a better life for me and my children and that means sometimes I lose time at the weekends etc.

Thinking about why you are pursuing this change, whatever it may be, will get you back on track and keep you there. Perhaps create a vision board of your future goals and dreams and this will be a great reminder to you. Especially if you are a visual person. Stick it up in your favourite place at home and regularly look at it!

Keep going

You will reach times when it is hard to keep taking the knock backs and carry on. Here is where resilience and pig-headedness will be your friends.

You may start to think the grass looks greener elsewhere and that plodding on in your old job with less money or a steady career was the best option after all. Now I am not here to tell you what to do, you need to do that yourself, but please do be honest and don't give up until you have really REALLY tried. It is usually darkest before dawn.

You will often feel like giving up because it is a way to end the hardship, but long term remember that it won't if you end up staying in a place you are unhappy.

Short term gain for long term pain is bad news.

Think about future you. What would they look back and say to present you? If they are in a better career/house/lifestyle (whatever YOUR vision is, no right or wrong here you might want to travel the world in a camper), they will look back and thank present you for staying the course. For not giving up. For grafting when you needed to, for taking chances and for making big sacrifices and decisions.

You don't want future you to look back and say, WHY THE HELL DIDN'T I STICK TO IT AND MAKE THAT MOVE WHEN I COULD? Now it is never too late to change career or path, but it can become difficult with age, let's be realistic. So, the sooner you start the better.

Age need never hold you back, you are only too old if you think you are! But one never knows what the future holds so waiting too long can mean time runs out for you. The best time to start is now.

Why is it so hard?

Why is it so hard? Well, it might not be.

Honestly you might find your path and grab an opportunity, or a spoon as Ross in Friends would say, and get your dream job or goal fast! But chances are you won't.

Change takes time, not only for you and your mindset and the time to make adaptations to your life and finances possibly etc, but you may have to study or gain experience through volunteering. Or work longer hours for a period. So don't expect overnight success, remember it is a long term plan presumably, so it will be worth the investment or time and possibly money to get you there.

It is also challenging because it not only takes time but energy. Both mentally and physically you will probably be put through the ringer, and you need to be ready for that. Nothing good comes easy though, does it?

Some people thrive in change, they really do. So, you may relish the upheaval and the focus on a new goal and really get stuck in. With a clear plan it is much easier to manage that. If you do struggle though, you won't be alone.

I hate change in many ways, I got a new phone and it took me four plus months to change over to it. Ridiculous!! I am a kick-ass businesswoman who can't change her phone over.

But why not? Well, it is the fear, of course. The fear of it all going horribly wrong! If you are an overthinker like me, this fear can become paralysing. I have worked on this a fair bit and actually the phone thing was a turning point for me, and I used it to learn a lot about myself! But fear can stop us doing so much.

The fear of failing at this new quest for a career of your dreams may well give you a serious headache.

Fear of the unknown

It is not only a fear of failure giving you a kicking though, what about the fear of the unknown? I have talked about visualising a future where things are how you want them. But it is still an unknown until you get there.

The problem with humans and the unknown is our brains are so clever and busy they fill that unknown up with lots of ideas. Usually bad ones. The unknown gets coloured in and often by fears, previous experiences and expectations. Not always good ones!

Some people may be what is termed a natural worrier where negativity seems to dog you however fast you run. It has to be said though, I don't think you are necessarily naturally prone to this, and it is probably conditioning, which is all perfectly undoable. Brains can be retrained, it just takes consistency.

You may need expert help with that or be able to do it yourself by using daily gratitude practise, self-care as mentioned previously, positive affirmations, meditation, whatever works for you. Don't just accept you are a worrier or overthinker and that is your lot in life. Sure, there are some traits we are better off accepting but generally patterns of thinking are changeable. Please do seek professional help if needed though.

The more positive your mindset the better, and then hopefully your brain won't paint the worst-case scenario every time. You control your thoughts remember, honest! So, if you get that negative trickle and the fear starts to creep in, have a reset.

Logically think it through and remind yourself that there is no point wasting energy on things that haven't and may not happen and think about how amazing that future could be!

Face those fears though, don't bury them.

What's the worst that could happen?

Whilst I have said don't paint the worst-case scenario all the time, actually thinking about it and working through it can take the fear out of it. And help stop it repeatedly coming back into your head.

We all know trying to hide a thought away just means it'll rear its ugly head later, usually when we are trying to sleep!

You can't hide from thoughts; trust me I have tried, and it doesn't work. It actually gives them more fuel somehow! Fearful ones especially thrive on being hidden and start to build up into seemingly insurmountable heights. The good news is that letting them out and letting the daylight shine onto them will shrivel them up like vampires, and you can add some logic to the mix.

Talking about those worst-case scenarios, and then reasoning out what would happen or how you could deal with it will sap their power over you. You can also think rationally about the chances of it happening, and about whether it is worse not to try at all.

What happens if you do nothing? A life of misery, boredom or mediocrity continues. Yawn.

What if the worst thing to happen is that you do nothing at all, and everything stays the same? Trying and failing will suck … but you regretting things you didn't do is often a lot worse than regretting things you did. When it comes to career choices anyway!

Change of mentality and how to embrace it

Sometimes we psych ourselves out without even realising it and what you need to do here is address the fears you have about what will stop you succeeding.

With the greatest will in the world, we live in a society that isn't always inclusive of diversity, so perhaps you are worried about your age or your gender holding you back or even your sexuality.

One of the things I talk extensively about in this book is the strength you all have in being yourself and being real, and I stand by this. You're only too old for something if you think you are, it is also illegal for someone to discriminate against you for any of the above reasons including disability and race.

However, as we've said this is not a perfect world and discrimination does happen, so please remember to keep your age, gender, sexuality, disability and race away from your CV, it has no place on there in the UK or the US.

Obviously, people can work things out from names, length of experience or other areas on your CV, but there is no need to give that information away so clearly. There is no need to include dates on education for example and no need to mention where you were born et cetera.

But the most important thing here is your own mentality, you cannot change someone else's view and if a company wants to discriminate against you, they will. This is not right (actually it is one of the things that makes me most angry in life!) however, do you want to work for a company that has that view anyway. No, of course you don't.

Be yourself and be proud of who you are but also believe that you are good enough. Address those fears head on like we've said before. Why do you think you're too old for something? Look up stories of older people getting their degrees or doing amazing feats and remind yourself that age is just a number. Read inspiring stories of transgender people paving the way in an industry, look up the female CEOs kicking ass. Search out the first black woman to run a bank.

Believe it can be done! You are unique and kick-ass at what you do, and that is more important than your age, gender, sexuality, disability, race or anything else, believe that and others will too. Generally speaking, one of the biggest things that will get in your way when trying to move on and get a new job will be you.

Why will it be worth it?

Keep your eyes on the prize! Remind yourself of why you are doing it, then remind yourself again. Make that vision board of your future dreams and goals and pin it up. Make sure you tap into those feelings of hope and envision crossing that finish line. Great athletes use visualisation to help them win races and I think it can help for anything.

Picture yourself in that new job and thriving in your new lifestyle, whatever that may be. Think about the opportunities you will be able to give your children, for example, if you are earning more money or have more freedom and time for them. Or perhaps you want to move to a new area which will provide a better quality of life for you or your family. However your future looks to you, really immerse yourself in that vision and really believe you can get there.

Picture yourself in the future looking back on today, the day you made the decision to make a change. The day you decided to make a difference for yourself and gifted yourself the future you really wanted.

It will be hard work, let's not kid ourselves, usually a change is work and can be stressful, that is why it is essential to think about the positives of getting to your end goal. Staying focused on what you are doing and why you are doing it will help you get through the hardest times, because some days it may feel like it's just too much or you have made a bad decision, and you need something to get you through those days.

Don't burn out

It may be hard work at times, you might be putting in extra hours studying alongside your current role or even doing two jobs or volunteering on top of a full-time job. Whatever the pressure looks like to you when making this career change it can be easy to burn out. If you go too hard, too fast you will end up failing, because you won't keep up the pace.

Please remember the self-care we have spoken about already and look after yourself. No one can maintain a hardcore approach all the time, everyone needs a break, so make sure you listen to yourself. Listen to your body and take breaks when you need to.

Job seeking itself can feel like a full-time job at times but it's still important to have breaks and give yourself a day off or weekend with your family or friends etc. If you have regular breaks, you will come back fighting and be in a far better position than you were before.

It's always a good idea to renew your energy as it is a cliché, but you can't pour from an empty cup, and you will be no use to anyone if you completely burn out and don't make it to the end of this journey into a new career/role.

It should also be noted here that you must remember to enjoy the journey, even the hard bits will help you grow strong and resilient and will help you appreciate the easier times. Everything in life and life itself is a journey. Although in this case the destination is important, as it's your new job role or new career, the journey is still part of your life so don't make it so brutal that you feel like giving up every day or you make yourself physically or mentally ill.

When to rethink your strategy

I nearly called this part when to give up but that would be a little too negative. Hopefully, you won't find that you need to give up at any point. However, please be aware you may have chosen something that just doesn't work for you or becomes impossible for whatever reason.

An example of this might be you need to retrain and do an access course in order to do a degree, but when it comes to the study it turns out it's beyond your capability and you just can't do it. This of course would be a shame, but shit happens, and it will just mean that that journey is not for you after all.

It may not be an end to your career aspirations completely, you may just need to adjust them. It may be the case that you can't reach the level in a role that you wanted to, for example you want to be a teacher but you can't do the right study to get there, however, you may be able to train as a teaching assistant or work in some other role in education.

There will be other options open to you. If the passion is there for a particular sector or a particular type of role then keep your mind open. If it becomes difficult to achieve what you wanted, reassess and create a new goal.

I worked as an education ranger for a nature reserve and it was in essence an unqualified teaching role, you never know what is out there! I got the role by volunteering first so I proved that I could do it.

Knowing when to give up is itself a strength, so don't be afraid to make that decision if it feels absolutely right. You will know if it does because you'll make it and you will feel a great sense of relief.

Perhaps you need a new strategy or approach to what you're doing. If, for example, you changed your CV and sent it out and just can't get any interviews for what you want to do then maybe you need help with your CV or maybe you need to do extra training to gain skills in order to get those interviews. There is no need to give up completely, just rethink your strategy and come up with a new way to get to your goal. Knowing when to ask for help is a skill.

CHAPTER 9
KNOW YOUR WORTH/STEPPING UP A LEVEL

Act the part

In order to step up a level at work, you must address your mindset. Start acting like you are already in that position of leadership. Because if you don't believe in yourself then neither will anyone else.

You need to be able to change your mindset and think like you're in that better position. Now I don't mean going around bossing everyone about and stepping on a manager's toes. What I mean is going the extra mile and doing things unpaid, staying late and supporting people around you. If you want to be a leader, then act like one. The actions you show, and therefore how you're perceived by others in the workplace are essential here.

It's easier to show you have the skills that are needed if you can demonstrate them. They will get recognised, hopefully, plus you'll be able to use them as examples as you create your CV and in interviews. Whereas if you're not doing these things, then you can't use them as examples. Good solid examples of actually developing people will stand you in much better stead, than if you've done a course in management or coaching.

Obviously if you're somewhere where that's not appreciated it's something you need to think about. Still, it might be worth that short term sacrifice of doing it without any appreciation for the long term career move, so you can use it as evidence for an interview elsewhere.

Run your own race

The dangers of comparing yourself with other people are extensive, just don't do it. You may know people who have excelled in their careers, seemingly moving up the ranks without batting an eyelid whilst you graft away at the bottom. Whatever it is, it's unlikely you know the whole story for a start and also that person isn't you. Run your own race.

What you need to do is swap self-comparison with self-compassion. You've been doing your best with the situation you are in, and you can't go back and change what's happened anyway so forget regrets and keep focused on the present and the future. We can learn from history, but it is dangerous to dwell there very long as you lose your perspective and hope.

The wonder of social media means we get to see what everyone else is doing all the time. You can usually see what someone had for breakfast or where they spent their weekend. What you must remember is we don't see everything. And we don't see the bad bits, usually. That is why comparing yourself online is even more futile than doing it in real life.

The joy of a platform like LinkedIn is we can network with businesspeople all over the world, and trust me, I love to do just that, and I've met some incredible people. The downside is people are not always accurate in their presentation of themselves, there is a lot of bullshit on this platform and often you can see right through it, but sometimes we don't and it can appear that people are far more successful than they actually are. So just remember that everything you see online isn't real life. Try and be yourself in your posts or comments online, so you don't fall into the same trap.

Let your numbers talk

Keep a track of numbers. Stats and metrics from the things you have involvement in. Quantifiable achievements are so powerful, and they can really show what impact you have had in a role.

An example of what I mean could be improved sales year on year or money that has been saved due to an initiative you led. Putting these figures in your CV will really show you can prove your track record of success.

Some jobs are harder than others to track, but remember things like budgets you have managed, number of people in the team you led, number of views on social media marketing, number of customers through the door, reduced turnover of staff, projects completed. It could be anything.

Try not to worry about claiming you did things if it was a team effort, especially if you led the team. Yes, be accurate and state it was a team set up but if you were a member or led a team that had a success then you have every right to talk about that on your CV. Obviously avoid any false claims that could get you in hot water.

Beware of NDA situations and it may be that you are able to put figures onto your CV but not on a public domain like LinkedIn. Especially if you have turned a business around, they may not want you to shout about the fact that they were making a loss!

If you are in this situation then make sure you are in control of where your CV goes, don't post it on lots of job boards.

What do people say?

Most of us find it quite hard to be really positive about ourselves, especially in writing. To be honest I probably wouldn't have a job as a CV writer if people were really good at this because the profile statement at the beginning is the bit people struggle with the most. Even with a good layout for your CV and advice on how to do it, it can still be hard to nail that personal statement at the beginning.

But it's essential you do nail this part of your CV and it will actually help you present yourself better in interviews. Just in general it will boost your confidence no end if you are able to write a positive and truthful summary of your skills and experience and explain why you do what you do.

So, why not think about what other people say about you. Now I don't mean anything bad of course, don't listen at closed doors you won't hear anything good, trust me. What I mean is think back to appraisals, for example, what has been said about you in the workplace? What positive feedback have you had from a manager? What have clients said about you? What have colleagues said about you? Perhaps you have recommendations on somewhere like LinkedIn or perhaps you will actually have to ask people in person what they think. Don't be scared to ask people, most people are more than happy to give some feedback and you might be surprised by what you hear!

More often than not, people have a much better view of us than we do of ourselves, especially if you've been struggling with any confidence issues. Sometimes people notice things about the way we do a job that we don't notice ourselves or we just take for granted. So, getting an objective view of your own abilities can be quite helpful.

You may have had an analysis done on your management style or had a personality test or any other kind of psychometric testing, these are all useful as well. Although please do take some of those with a pinch of salt they are not the be all and end all.

But do listen to those supportive people who want the best for you. Listen to what people say and take it on board as long as they are people with your best interests at heart. At the end of the day, the decisions and the hard work will be down to you but having someone in your corner will definitely make the journey a lot easier.

Your impact

One thing to consider when writing a CV or approaching a career or job change is the impact you've had in your roles. If you can get this across on your CV it will have a great effect on the person who reads it.

What I mean by this is not just thinking about the things you did everyday but the effect those things had on the business or on the clients or on your colleagues. So don't just list all the responsibilities you had, especially if many of them are expected responsibilities for a set role. Think about the things you did that set you apart and the things you did that actually had an impact.

It may be that you had an influence on the business as a whole, its sales, its growth, its processes, its people, IT systems, its customers. Whatever it is, think about it in terms of numbers as much as you can. Think about what would have happened if you weren't there, what difference have you actually made by being in your role.

Thinking about your impact can actually have a positive effect on your confidence levels as well reminding you that you did actually make a difference even if the job ended up becoming miserable or the culture turned bad, perhaps you had a really good relationship with the customers so you can remember that as a worthwhile part of the role.

I know that when I worked in advertising it ended on a sour note for me because I didn't agree with some of the decisions that were being made, however, my clients really appreciated me. I actually left them quite sad when I moved on and they sent me emails supporting and congratulating me and thanking me for all my help. This reminded me that the job wasn't all bad after all and in fact, I had really helped the clients and made their lives easier, which was the main point of my job anyway. I am still really glad I left though!

Getting the seniority into your CV

Think about what you are putting in and what you might want to leave out. Some clear areas of leadership are the ability to create strategies and think about the big picture but also the ability to lead people.

Talking about the type of leader you are is essential if you are going for a role that involves leadership. How you manage people and how you are perceived as a leader is really important to get across on a CV, don't expect people to make assumptions.

Adding a sense of scale can be good for this if you've led teams of people put the numbers in. Think about your style of leadership, there are many different ways to lead. Are you collaborative? Do you help develop people? Do you have a coaching or mentoring style? Do you empower people and let them get on with it or are you more authoritative?

There are also things that you might add on your CV that downgrade your seniority in some way, which might sound weird, but let me explain.

I have mentioned this already but things like GCSEs or the ability to use Microsoft Word or other basic skills or software are unnecessary once you reach a certain level. Unless you're a school leaver or you're going for a basic position that requires you to indicate you have GCSEs or your A levels then you don't need to put these on, especially if you have a degree and/or career experience. They don't need to know which school you went to or if you got a D in RE.

Once you reach a certain level in office-based work, being able to use Microsoft Office is an assumption people will happily make and frankly you don't need to tell them unless it's in the job spec. Including it can suggest you find it difficult to focus on the correct things or don't rate yourself highly enough, so think about your CV objectively and whether it is senior enough.

Case Study
Don't Undermine Yourself

Alan is a seriously skilled Engineering Manager, but his CV was 6 pages of courses from the 90s and GCSEs and other old information. All of which wasted space and undermined his seniority.

We worked together on his CV and LinkedIn and by the time we were finished he had 2 pages that summed him up perfectly and got him more interviews than he could shake a stick at! Never before had his CV got that much attention, was what he said.

In his own words:
"After a couple of months job searching and not a lot happening, decided to get advice on my CV. Rebecca was recommended to me so decided to bite the bullet. I now have a Kiss-ass CV and within a couple of days I am starting to get noticed and people contacting me!! - that's a first. Money well spent and highly recommend anyone else struggling to seek her advice. Thank you Rebecca 'Kick-ass' Pay."

He accepted a great offer and now has a CV that he can just adjust as his career continues, 6 pages of everything you have ever done is never needed!

Find your weak spots

No one is brilliant at everything, there may be some areas you need to improve and being honest with yourself about this is really important.

Firstly, compare your skill set to a job description of a role that you want to go for eventually. What gaps do you have and what areas do you need to improve?

There may be specific and obvious things such as qualifications in which case you can create a plan in order to gain those at work or in your own time. Other things may be related to skills you need to gain in the workplace such as leadership or organisation. Be honest with yourself here and think about which areas you struggle with or look back at appraisals and see which were identified as areas that needed work.

Knowing your weak spots is actually a huge strength and working on them will enable you to become a more rounded person and prepare you for the next role. There's no point blagging your way into a new role if you really don't have the skills to deal with it. Having the confidence to be able to learn something on the job is one thing, jumping feet first into a management role with zero experience is quite another.

How to upskill

As we have discussed, you may need to upskill at some point it may be that there are certain skills you need to gain in order to change careers or move up in a role. There are multiple ways to do this and I will discuss a few here.

Firstly, there is the more obvious choice of taking actual courses or doing training or education in some way. For example, in project management you may need Agile PM or PRINCE2 for a role so you can study and complete the relevant one. Some courses may be expensive or may take a long time so this is something you need to weigh up as to how important it definitely is.

There may be some skills you can gain from taking on extra responsibilities at work, we have covered this previously but perhaps doing things unpaid or offering to help a different department.

There may even be a chance of secondment to a new area in order to upskill yourself. This is something that's always worth looking into, especially if you work for a large company. Many companies offer this as part of a training and development programme obviously some may not, but it doesn't hurt to ask.

Volunteering is another great way to gain skills outside of your main job, charities are always looking for people to help them in various areas. For example, I worked for the Citizen Advice Bureau voluntarily every week in marketing, helping with a campaign. This is something I did whilst working full-time at the council and it meant spending a few hours every week doing this but it really helped upskill me in a different area and also enabled me to meet new people and develop a new network. Volunteering also makes you feel good about making a difference when a paycheck isn't involved.

It's not all about money

Moving up a level at work usually involves a pay increase and that may be the case for you, which is great, more responsibility should definitely incur a greater financial reward. However, sometimes the measure of a role is how it makes you feel, not how it grows your bank balance.

Yes, we all need money to live, and I will be the first to tell you that you can have a comfortable lifestyle and do something you love/makes a difference. But when thinking about moving up at work, remember that you don't HAVE to move up just because it's the next logical step.

As you get promoted you sometimes end up moving away from the parts of the job you actually loved in the first place! If you are really lucky you evolve with the role and learn to love training others or managing them doing the roles you once did. That isn't always the case though and if you don't want to move into managing people, that's okay.

Be honest with yourself about what you DO want and it'll be easier to choose that next step. Doing things because we think we have to or even perhaps because we haven't thought about an alternative is not the best way to make decisions.

Another factor may be an option to take on more responsibility without any additional remuneration. If that is the situation then you need to weigh up the benefit of the potential experience vs the extra time and stress you might incur.

As a short-term step towards a long term goal I think it is worth considering, if you don't have the long term plan in place then be very careful as you will end up feeling bitter and overworked.

Changing your mind isn't a weakness

We all know women have the prerogative to change their minds. Well, guess what? Everyone does.

Maybe you studied for years or made a big deal about your career choices or maybe you just fell into it, whichever it is you are allowed to change your mind.

For goodness' sake, don't carry on with something because you are too worried about what others might think if you change your mind.

This reminds me of a scene in Peep Show, if you're not a fan I apologise, if you are then yay! Mark is going to propose to Sophie, but goes for a long walk and changes his mind, he is elated he doesn't actually have to go through with something that was clearly going to make him miserable. But in the meantime, she finds the ring ... so rather than telling her the truth he accepts her yes to his indirect proposal.

Jez, the other main character, asks Mark if he is really going to go through with being married to someone for the rest of his life just to avoid social embarrassment of telling her he changed his mind, and Mark says, yes, he is.

It seems ridiculous (and hilarious by the way) in the scenario, but the fact is people often seem to end up in these situations. If you are prone to people pleasing this could be you. Ending up in a job or even a marriage due to parental or other people's influence/approval. It's not really great, is it ...

You only get one life (rumour has it) so let's not waste too much of it doing things that other people want us to do. The happier you are, the lovelier you will be to be around and the more of a positive influence you can have on others.

CHAPTER 10
HOPE FOR THE FUTURE – A SUMMARY

So here we are, the end of the book. Well done, you made it through and hopefully gained lots of knowledge you will now put to use. And that is the key here, *you need to take action*.

Here is a summary of each chapter and the key takeaway points!

Chapter 1 What Job Do You REALLY Want - Pivot Into Perfection

Deciding on the job you want, opening your mind to any possibility and getting deep about your beliefs and ethos are all vital. Work out what the ideal role is then research and plan how to achieve that goal.

Chapter 2 Structure – 'The Perfect CV'

All the key ways to structure a CV for applying for jobs in the standard way. The main points being to keep it simple and easy to read and focus it on what you have achieved and showcase your highlights.

Chapter 3 Mistakes and No-Nos

Don't overshare or complicate it with fancy graphics, photos, boxes, columns, etc. unless you are applying direct and a creative.

Chapter 4 Tailor and Tweak

Adapt your CV for every application, don't send the same one to every role and expect to get shortlisted! Work out what your USP is and get some personality into the CV.

Chapter 5 Making LinkedIn Work for You

Start by setting up a killer profile, getting the banner and photo right and a tagline that tells people what you do.

Then get that About section to do the work and convince people you know what you're talking about by focusing on your skills and achievements but making sure it showcases you in an interesting way.

Posting and commenting can be strong ways to build a supportive and useful network that may create opportunities for you.

Chapter 6 Find Them and Follow Up

Get to the decision-makers, build up rapport and use some fun or bold ways to get their attention.

Chapter 7 You Don't Need to Ask Permission From ANYONE (But Give It to Yourself)

Stop making excuses and take action! Acknowledge what your roadblocks are and get past them. Envision that future in the right job and it will help you make it a reality. Remind yourself about the price of doing nothing, it will all stay the same.

Chapter 8 Feel the Fear and Do It Anyway

It will be scary to make a change but that doesn't mean you can't do it. Realising you will get rejected and have doubts and will need to stay determined and strong is half the battle! Get that mindset on track and also remember it might not work but you know you will have tried your best.

Chapter 9 Know Your Worth/Stepping Up a Level

If you are hoping to move up or get a new job, then knowing the impact you have at work is vital. It is also important to have an awareness of where you have skill gaps and how to fill them. Also, let go of any expectations you had of a planned out career and remember it is okay to change your mind and follow a new path.

My wish for you is hope for your future and the knowledge that you CAN get that job you really want. It doesn't have to stay a dream, it can be a reality. But please don't kid yourself, just reading this book won't get you anywhere. Take action to decide on what you want to do, create a plan for how you're going to get there and build the CV and LinkedIn strategy that works for you. Otherwise, you will stay exactly where you are now. Which I assume is somewhere you don't want to be since you bought this book.

Think about when you're sitting in your rocking chair, old and wizened, what will you be looking back on in your life? Maybe a family, thinking fondly of some of the fun experiences you had, but hopefully zero regrets about what you spent a lot of your time doing, and that means your work.

So, please go onwards with confidence and a smile on your face, but get ready for some hard work. I would love to hear from any of you that take action and in fact make a change, why not tag me on Twitter or LinkedIn? Seeing clients change their lives around is why I do what I do in the first place. But ultimately, there is only one person who you need to do this for, and that's you.

Don't forget to check out my website to get my kick-ass CV template for FREE and sign up to my mailing list if you want to get regular tips.

Stay positive, get a plan, look after yourself along the way and go get the future you actually want, it's in your hands. Go kick some ass!

ABOUT THE AUTHOR

Rebecca Pay is known for creating kick-ass CVs and supporting people who want to make a career change or step up into a new role by instilling confidence and empowering people to take the leap. She is the creator of the Kick-ass CV method, follow #KickassCVs for tips.

With a background that includes recruitment, advertising, sales, hospitality, education and proofreading she has a wealth of knowledge and experiences to draw from. But her real skill is that she makes people feel at ease and can make friends with nearly anyone.

This has enabled her to grow a network on and offline and it also leaves clients feeling like they're truly supported, with someone in their corner.

She is based in Coventry in the middle of the UK, but was born in Devon, and being by the sea is one of her favourite places. As a mum of two young children, one of whom is neurodiverse, and the founder of The Pay It Forward Enterprise (providing free CV/career support to those made redundant in 2020), she likes to keep busy!

Her following on LinkedIn would also say she is known for ice cream selfies and being the only CV writer who can pole dance, due to her love of pole fitness. She also shares insights about her journey as a parent and valuable CV and LinkedIn tips.

Not your average writer, and this is not an average book.

* * *

I would love to know what you thought of this book! You can write a review with your thoughts at:

- Amazon – search for *How to get the kick-ass career you deserve*

- Goodreads – search for Rebecca Pay

- Facebook – search for Pay for Precision Proofreading

Links and how to contact me

Come and grab some free stuff! As a reader (and hopefully purchaser) of this book you get access to some cool stuff, not least of all my kick-ass CV template. So, click (or type out if you're reading the printed version) the link below and check it out.

Website: www.payforprecision.com

I will happily answer DMs or you can contact me through my page, but LinkedIn is where I am most active.

LinkedIn: https://www.linkedin.com/in/payforprecision/

Facebook: https://www.facebook.com/PayforPrecision

Twitter: https://twitter.com/PayforPrecision

Instagram: https://www.instagram.com/payforprecision/

ACKNOWLEDGEMENTS

Firstly, thanks to me for actually writing this book and my coach Dan Meredith for bullying me into doing it!

Secondly, thanks to my husband Dave and my children Hannah and Max for putting up with me working late and at weekends to get this finished, I know it was annoying, so I appreciate it!

Thirdly, big shout outs to the beta readers who kindly gave me feedback on the first draft, it was valuable and I appreciate you all: Harry Whitcher, Hayley Hudson, Kate Howden, Michael Simmons, Richard Cook, Giulio Virduci and David Pay.

Thanks to Kirsten Rees for being brave enough to edit and proofread a book for a trained editor and proofreader! Thanks especially to Adam Stevens for the hard work on the website, which dragged me out of procrastination hell and pushed me into actually having one after over seven years!

Thanks to the ice cream and snacks for getting me through and the friends in my corner who always have my back. You know who you are, I love you all.